Dear Human at the Edge of Time

POEMS ON CLIMATE CHANGE IN THE UNITED STATES

Dear Human at the Edge of Time

Poems on Climate Change in the United States

A COMPANION TO THE FIFTH
NATIONAL CLIMATE ASSESSMENT

Edited by

Luisa A. Igloria, Aileen Cassinetto & Jeremy S. Hoffman

Foreword by Claire Wahmanholm

Paloma Press

Copyright © 2023 by Luisa A. Igloria, Aileen I. Cassinetto & Jeremy S. Hoffman for the authors. Copyrights revert to the authors on publication.

Library of Congress Cataloging-in-Publication Data

Names: Igloria, Luisa A., editor. | Hoffman, Jeremy S., editor. |
    Cassinetto, Aileen I., editor.
Title: Dear human at the edge of time : poems on climate change in the
    United States / Luisa A. Igloria, Jeremy S. Hoffman, Aileen I.
    Cassinetto, editors.
Description: First. | San Mateo, California : Paloma Press, 2023. |
    Summary: "Dear Human at the Edge of Time" is an additional opportunity
    for U.S.-based poets to participate in the Fifth National Climate
    Assessment (NCA5) by sharing our communities' stories of climate change
    alongside this scientific information. This anthology features poems by
    over 70 poets addressing the theme of urgency from climate impacts in
    the poets' immediate experience and/or community/region"
    ~ Provided by publisher.
Identifiers: LCCN 2023009083 | ISBN 9781734496543 (paperback)
Subjects: LCSH: American poetry~21st century. | Climatic changes~Poetry.
    | Global warming~Poetry. | LCGFT: Poetry.
Classification: LCC PS595.C554 D43 2023 | DDC 811/.6~dc23/eng/20230804
LC record available at https://lccn.loc.gov/2023009083

Book Design by C. Sophia Ibardaloza

ALL RIGHTS RESERVED

Except for brief passages quoted for review or critical purposes, no part of this book may be reproduced or transmitted in any form or by any means, electronic or mechanical, including photocopying, recording, or by any information storage and retrieval system, without the proper written permission of the copyright owner unless such copying is expressly permitted by federal copyright law. With the exception of nonprofit transmission in Braille, Paloma Press is not authorized to grant permission for further uses of copyrighted selections reprinted in this book without the permission of their owner. Permission must be obtained from the copyright owner as identified herein.

PALOMA PRESS
San Mateo & Morgan Hill, California
www.palomapress.org

Printed in the United States of America

"I can tell you a lot about your 'vulnerability' to climate change just by knowing your zip code. Climate change simply amplifies the background hum of inequity in our world."
—Dr. Jeremy S. Hoffman, Chapter Lead for the Southeast, Fifth National Climate Assessment (NCA5)

CONTENTS

FOREWORD

by Claire Wahmanholm

MY THIRD COLLECTION, *Meltwater*, came out earlier this spring, and I have spent the last several months promoting it— reading in bookstores, bars, gardens, galleries; at universities and conferences; outside beside a frozen lake. I have answered questions about it, read poems from it, designed craft talks and poetry prompts around it. These events have brought me into contact with a wonderful community of readers and writers, but they have also been exhausting. I love my book, but my own ecopoetry is grim, anxious, dystopian. Fear is the axis on which it spins. It is a poetry of mourning, of preparing for inevitable disaster. I identify with the speaker of Caitlin Gildrien's "Baseline": "It doesn't seem like you should be able/ to hold panic like a too-full cup/ all day. But all day it sloshes/ and slips inside of me." To climb inside of my own voice time and time again and peer out from its jaws has been claustrophobic, occasionally punishing. It made me wonder, as Karen Llagas writes in "Some conjunctions in our late anthropocene," "[i]f there's more to do// than practice looking at the sun."

What a balm, then, to encounter this anthology at the end of that season. What a relief to the eyes to gaze up at a constellation-studded sky. In all things, not just poetry, it is imperative that we get outside of ourselves and our one version of events. We will not survive this crisis without it.

This is not to say I didn't recognize my own tendencies in some of these poems. There is despair, anger, anxiety, cynicism. In some poems, mourning floods its banks. Other poems anticipate— sometimes stoically, sometimes gleefully—our demise. Many cup a hand around the beauty of the world even as the wind of annihilation gusts toward it. Some poems were so poignant I could taste blood in my mouth. I felt at home in their worlds.

But in other of these poems, hope, grace, determination, and redemption hold their ground. And it was while reading these that I felt most challenged, even chastened.

"Dear human at the edge of time," writes Cassandra Bousquet in the anthology's title poem. "The edge is not the end. We still have time to try."

The first time I read these lines, I paused, wary. Skeptical. Disbelieving, even. How is an edge *not* an end?

The word *edge* comes from the Old English *ęcg*, which meant *edge* of course, but also *corner* or *point*. I have a mind that turns each edge into the edge of a knife; each corner into a place to be cornered; each point into a point of no return.

But rather than teetering on a knife's edge, why not picture our toes gripping the ledge above a rich, warm sea? Why not imagine ourselves on the brink of possibility instead of doom? Do we want to turn back around—back toward capitalism, individualism, unchecked growth and consumption—back toward what is familiar but what will surely destroy us? Or do we want to leap?

This poem is—as all good poems are—an invitation to reimagine the relationship between the self and words; between the self and the world.

So I held *edge* in my mind and let it soften into the image of an ecotone: an area of transition, of permeability. *Ecotone*, from the Greek *oikos* (home) and *tonus* (tension). A diverse, fertile area where two biomes overlap (mangrove forests, estuaries, treelines, floodplains, marshes); whose inhabitants must thrive under a wide variety of conditions; whose inhabitants are thereby primed for adaptation and endurance. Within the context of ecology, this interaction between habitats is known as an *edge effect*.

you need to learn how
to flow between ecstasy
and grief, between love
and the endangerment of love
so as to go on
and do the one thing
that needs to be done.
to give life
the one chance
it wants for itself:
to go on.

Susanne Moser, "extinction crisis"

Adaptation isn't an option for us, at least not in the same way. It's not something we can wait for, something we can just let happen to us. If we want to adapt—if we don't want the future to be a wasteland—we will need to work for it. We will need to be able to imagine different relationships between each other, between ourselves and capital, between ourselves and the non-human world. Maybe edges provide just enough urgency, just enough pressure, to spur us into flight:

When we tell the story
of how we survived the collapse,
we might say:

like birds, we learned
to move as one.
We grew lighter
and lengthened our wings.

Anna Sims Bartel, "When we tell the story"

Moving as one. Growing lighter. Lengthening our wings. What might this look like for us humans? For poets like Cindy Veach and Anna Sims Bartel, it looks like taking our cues from the animal world, which exists in right relation to the earth by using only what it needs. For Lesley Wheeler it's the certainty of being held by the earth, of knowing that "something animate, / mycelial [...] touches me back." It looks like the warmth of compromise, agreement, and beneficence for Ellen Taylor.

For some poets, like Luisa A. Igloria, Eileen R. Tabios, and Eric Forsbergh, it looks like memorializing specific climate-related disasters. For poets like Rajiv Mohabir it means naming and rejecting the specific poisons of capitalism. For Erika Spanger it means "fighting like hell" for what's still beautiful.

Again and again, poets turn to joy—Mary Grace Bertulfo's long-awaited family reunion; Molly Fisk's sandhill cranes; Kindra McDonald's yellow warblers; January Gill O'Neil's late-season cherry tomatoes—or if not joy, maybe something closer to awe, like Brian Turner's grove of redwoods or Kate Cell's New England anemone.

For poets like Mark Spitzer and Caitlin Gildrien, it means acknowledging the sheer improbability of being here at all. It looks like prayer for Denise Wilcox. And for Brian Sonia-Wallace it means trusting that something—even if it isn't us—will survive the fire.

An anthology like this represents just a sliver of people who are deeply invested in this work. For every poet in this anthology—each of whom care desperately about the world and what we are doing to it—there are approximately 2,500,739 people in the United States[1] —some poets, but mostly not—who feel the same way: that we are in serious trouble; that greed has brought us here; that we love the world and think it is worth saving; that we are willing to reimagine our societies in order to do it.

And this is only one anthology. In the past five years alone, eco anthologies have been published all over the world: some focus on a specific state[2], region[3], country[4] (including diasporic communities[5]), or culture[6]; some were written in response to a particular natural disaster[7]; some are written by children[8]; some pull us into the future[9]; some are furious and grim[10], while others are committed to hope[11]. More will come next year. There will never be too many.

I have not met even 3% of the poets included in this anthology, but we are gathered together here in poetic kinship. Moving as one. Growing lighter. Lengthening our wings. With the time we have.

May this anthology hold you, even as you—dear human at the edge of time—hold it in your hands.

Claire Wahmanholm is a contributing poet to this anthology, and also winner of the 2022 Montreal International Poetry Prize.

1 Marlon, Jennifer, et al. "Yale Climate Opinion Maps 2021." Yale Program on Climate Communication, 23 February 2022, climatecommunication.yale.edu/visualizations-data/ycom-us/. Accessed 25 June 2023.

2 For anthologies that focus on specific states, see Gibson, Margaret, ed. *Waking Up to the Earth: Connecticut Poets in a Time of Global Climate Crisis*. West Hartford: Grayson Books, 2021; Fisk, Molly, ed. *California Fire & Water: A Climate Crisis Anthology*. Nevada City: Story Street Press, 2020; Sterling, Meghan and Kathleen Sullivan, eds. *A Dangerous New World: Maine Voices on the Climate Crisis*. Portland: Littoral Books, 2019.

3 Hoerth, Katherine, ed. *Odes and Elegies: Eco-Poetry from the Texas Gulf Coast*. Beaumont: Lamar University Press, 2020.

4 For anthologies that focus on specific countries, see *Korean Green Literature: An Anthology of Seven Contemporary Eco-poets*. Seoul: International PEN-Korean Centre, 2020; Hamel, Jordan, et al, eds. *No Other Place to Stand: An Anthology of Climate Change Poetry from Aotearoa New Zealand*. Auckland: Auckland University Press, 2022; Sandilands, Catriona, ed. *Rising Tides: Reflections for Climate Changing Times*. British Columbia: Caitlin Press, 2019; Agrawal, Vinita, ed. *Open Your Eyes: an Anthology on Climate Change*. Calcutta: Hawakal Publishers, 2020.

5 Jetñil-Kijiner, Kathy, et al, eds. *Indigenous Pacific Islander Eco-Literatures*. Honolulu: University of Hawai'i Press, 2022.

6 Fraser, Jenny, ed. *Plant Power Sisterhood: an anthology of eco-revolution*. Baltimore: Akinoga Press, 2020.

7 Kaylock, Julia and Denise O'Hagan, eds. *Messages from the Embers: From Devastation to Hope: Australian Bushfire Poetry Anthology*. Sydney: Black Quill Press, 2020.

8 Lowther, Christine, ed. *Worth More Growing: Youth Poets and Activists Pay Homage to Trees*. British Columbia: Caitline Press, 2022.

9 Ward, A. R., ed. *Chlorophobia: An Eco-Horror Anthology*. Cambridgeshire: Ghost Orchid Press, 2021.

10 Rooney, Kathleen and Ashley Shelby, eds. *Undeniable: Writers Respond to Climate Change*. Louisville: Alternating Current, 2020.

11 Coleman, Elizabeth J., ed. *Here: Poems for the Planet*. Port Townsend: Copper Canyon Press, 2019.

INTRODUCTION

IN 2015, AROUND 50 words related to the natural world were removed from the Oxford Children's Dictionary. Robert MacFarlane lists some of the deleted words, including "acorn, adder, ash, beech, bluebell, buttercup, catkin, conker, cowslip, cygnet, dandelion, fern, hazel, heather, heron, ivy, kingfisher, lark, mistletoe, nectar, newt, otter, pasture, and willow. The words taking their places ... [include] attachment, block-graph, blog, broadband, bullet-point, celebrity, chatroom, committee, cut-and-paste, MP3 player and voice-mail." Well-known writers like Margaret Atwood and Andrew Motion started a campaign for the reinstatement of these words, and Robert Macfarlane put "The Lost Words" into a beautifully illustrated book for children. Clearly, the capacity to name and describe anything— not least of all the natural world—is connected to the idea of care and attention. And so, now, it seems even more important that we cultivate practices honoring our environment as well as language that will help us face the daily spectacle of global environmental degradations and arm us with a spirit of hope and agency.

When something dies or is taken away, we tend to want to memorialize it by building shrines, erecting headstones, creating simulacra. When what's taken away is something in the natural environment—what's been colonized, disappeared, or destroyed— we might rename the scars that are left "preservations." Not far from where I live, there's a popular theme park described as a place where "thrills and nature intersect." Millions of guests come annually to ride the rollercoasters, drink beer, eat themed cuisine, look at gray wolves, bald eagles, and other animals in the park's wildlife reserve section. In some way, such themed parks evoke World's Fairs, those grand universal exhibitions or expos meant to display the best or latest achievement of nations. In 1904 St. Louis, MO, this meant displaying more than a thousand Filipinos and other indigenous people in a live human zoo alongside the latest architecture and technology. The 422 acres of the nearby theme park are in James City County, near colonial Williamsburg. These lands were part of the original territory of the Powhatan people. Such displacements run throughout history; it's hard to think of anywhere now without considering who or what might have been there before anyone staked claims on it. And so, it's ironic that the park is divided into areas named after European countries—England, Scotland, Ireland, Italy, France, Germany.

The Roman poet Virgil, among the earliest to write in the pastoral tradition, was from a region in northern Italy where his father and other farmers were also nearly dispossessed of their land by Emperor Octavian. In north America, where indigenous peoples have lost almost all the land historically in their possession, accounts show that their relocations were usually to areas less viable to their way of life. The negative consequences of marginalizing policies continue into the present moment. Whatever names these go by (redlining, gentrification, land use and zoning regulations), their effects also put already disadvantaged communities at increased risk from climate change hazards.

This spring, in Norfolk, VA, community leaders from the south side of the Elizabeth River registered their displeasure at a meeting with the local Office of Resilience. They had learned of the city's proposal to raise houses and plant shorelines with natural grasses along their neighborhoods, while protective walls, berms, and levees were planned for the northside, benefiting wealthier communities (where there was also some concern that the height of the seawalls might compromise the beauty of the landscape). The information gathered by climate scientists shows it's more than just flooding that puts disadvantaged communities at risk—there's also a similar disparity in their vulnerability to extreme heat.

Climate scientists and researchers are working hard to gather and present quantitative data to make the case for taking climate action now. Where traditional pastorals have tended to idealize nature and country life, the ecopoetry we write today can offer another intimate barometer to show what is happening to a natural world on the brink of "climate midnight." This was the hope that led to this anthology of U.S.-based climate change poems. With my co-editors, I share the conviction that the stories we tell, from the ground of our living experience and stripped of jargon, are as important as science and policy in the race to communicate the urgency for collective climate action.

LUISA A. IGLORIA

JUNE IS LOW SEASON and monsoon where I grew up, wet with winds and storms and waist-deep floods. Before immigrating, I learned to yield to the archipelagic rhythms and torrents that beset Metropolitan Manila, one of the world's original global cities which linked Asia with the Spanish Americas.

June was also the start of the school year, when kids listened to the AM radio for storm warning signals: signal number three was for typhoons, and meant evacuation from low-lying or coastal areas; signal number two was for tropical storms, and meant classes were automatically suspended; signal number one was for tropical depressions, and meant donning our raincoats and braving scattered rains and near gale winds to go to class. Rising floodwaters was one of the main concerns, though a relatively new occurrence 40 years ago.

I first heard about climate change from my fifth grade social studies teacher who hailed from the same typhoon-prone island as my father. Connecting the dots between landslides and deforestation, and garbage pollution and greenhouse gases, she half-joked that thanks to human-induced weather changes, her tiny hometown, nearly 400 miles away from Manila, was only a category five tropical cyclone away from being wiped off the map. (She may also have alluded to colonialism's role in the Philippines' increasingly low forest cover, and indeed, the 2022 Intergovernmental Panel on Climate Change (IPCC) Sixth Assessment Report recognized colonialism as a major cause of the climate crisis, which continues to hinder the implementation of equitable solutions.)

Today, the Philippines is one of the places most vulnerable to sea level rise—same as my current hometown on the San Francisco Peninsula, bordered on either side by the San Francisco Bay and the Pacific Ocean, with the Santa Cruz Mountains running through it. I suppose it was inevitable that I would end up here, with the seawater in my veins, calling out to the mighty Pacific to find its way back to me.

They say that each of us contains the signature of everything that has ever been[1], all the bright things, and the good things, and the wretched and very human things. Across the San Francisco Bay Area, more than 5,200 toxic sites—some dating back to the 19th century—are at risk of coming into contact with rising groundwater caused by climate change, which means that "everything we've done in the past is coming up to haunt us."[2]

It wasn't so long ago that more than 300,000 prospectors rushed to California to earn a fortune. The quest for gold in the Old West forever changed the land—irreparably impacting local fauna and flora, impairing watersheds and food chains with mercury, and displacing Indigenous American communities that, precontact, lived sustainably for thousands of years. Their descendants, possessing the knowledge and pathways needed to rebuild ties between people and land, are a vital resource in envisioning a more viable and creative climate response.

In the same vein, poetry is how we move in this world in relation to others. We offer these poems as a way to connect, humanize our diverse stories, and inspire action. Within each poem are ecosystems of shared lives and their histories, burdens and shared hopes. Our contributors, teen poets Eva Chen (p. 46) and Cassandra Bousquet (p. 62), said it best:

> *...we are tethering at the edge of summer.../ if we stay here too long, we will erode with the mountains.../*
> *The edge is not the end. We still have time to try.*

AILEEN CASSINETTO

---

[1] Frank, Adam. "Scientists Found Ripples in Space and Time. And You Have to Buy Groceries." *The Atlantic*, 29 June 2023, https://www.theatlantic.com/science/archive/2023/06/universe-gravitational-waves-nanograv-discovery/674570/. Accessed 6 July 2023.

[2] Romero, Ezra David. "MAP: More Than 5,000 Toxic Sites Along SF Bay Threatened by Rising Groundwater, New Study Finds." *KQED*, 23 June 2023, https://www.kqed.org/science/1983106/map-more-than-5000-toxic-sites-along-sf-bay-are-threatened-by-rising-groundwater-new-study-finds. Accessed 6 July 2023.

POETRY HAS HELPED me understand climate science and share its conclusions with new audiences for many years. When I was a graduate student studying paleoclimatology at Oregon State University, I started writing poetry—specifically haiku—to help me digest and summarize landmark publications in my field of study while preparing for my comprehensive oral exams. Like many milestones along the winding path that leads to earning your Ph.D., these exams carry an immense amount of pressure and stress to perform at a high level—and as they should, since failing them could put your entire Ph.D. journey in jeopardy. I found that writing these brief yet dense poems provided a way to not only internalize some of the foundational knowledge relevant to my field, but also gave me an outlet for channeling my anxiety about the upcoming exams into a creative endeavor. Since that time, I have always sought ways to incorporate the fine arts—from music, to poetry, to theater, to even stand-up comedy—into how I communicate about climate science and continue to internalize the meaning of new scientific discoveries.

This approach, along with my research focus on how climate change disproportionately impacts our neighbors with fewer resources and a history of marginalization, has allowed me to collaborate with people all throughout the country on ways to empower, lift up, and center community voices in the process of building equitable climate resilience in new and creative ways. Just in the last five years, we've discovered so much about the disparity in climate risks that permeates our country's neighborhoods, rooted in a history of decisions being made by few to impact many, reverberating in the present day as pockets of heat illness, flood damage, and dirty air. These discoveries have galvanized community organizations and residents alike to join together to create new parks on empty parking lots, plant native trees to shade future generations, advocate for policy that prioritizes investment by need and history, and grow food and cohesion on vacant lots to reshape how local economies function. All over our country, amidst these perilous conditions, people are joining together to engage with climate science in new and exciting ways to build a sustainable future. These stories need creative outlets to be shared broadly, too.

As such, *Dear Human at the Edge of Time* began as a science communication experiment. It grew into the volume you see before you; an accompaniment, companion, and counterpart to the Fifth National Climate Assessment (NCA5). The NCA5 is a congressionally-mandated summary of the latest scientific literature on how climate change is accelerating the climate risks experienced across our great country. Many hundreds of scientists spent many thousands of hours working together to synthesize the latest research and conclusions about how climate change is impacting our country, its residents, and their day-to-day lives. I hope that these poems provide additional context to the findings presented in the NCA5 as well as some creative inspiration for you to engage with climate science in a new way in your own back yard.

JEREMY S. HOFFMAN

I.

ADA LIMÓN

And, Too, The Fox

Comes with its streak of red
flashing across the lawn, squirrel
bound and bouncing almost
as if it were effortless to hunt,
food being an afterthought or
just a little boring. He doesn't
say a word. Just uses those four
black feet to silently go about
his work, which doesn't seem
like work at all but play. Fox
lives on the edges, pieces together
a living out of leftovers and lazy
rodents too slow for the telephone
pole. He takes only what he needs
and lives a life that some might
call small, has a few friends, likes
the grass when it's soft and green,
never cares how long you watch,
never cares what you need
when you're watching, never cares
what you do once he is gone.

SUE DAVIS GABBAY

Morning Song

There was a time when daily
I woke to a sweet aubade
sung by an avian choir;
as the years passed
The aubade became a solo
then, one brave voice
with no song, just a call
despairing, Where are the birds?
Who will sing the morning in?
No answer to the call;
how loud the silence.

KATHARYN HOWD MACHAN

Wild Peacocks on the Loose

Like at Jeanne's.
Like before the hurricane
tore and flooded and buried and stripped.
Like when I visited her one March
and their good strong claws made love's own thunder
on her metal roof as they sought mates.
Like the colors in old fairy tales
princes and princesses wear to impress
each other, themselves, the writers of stories
who *ooh* over purple and *ah* over green
that shimmers amethyst emerald light
and watches with myth's deep blue eye
defying hands' transgression. Like
the early world, the one before houses,
before people learned how to cage:
God's brilliant birds who know how to flee
when oceans rise in retribution,
when black winds roar in rage.

KAREN LLAGAS

Some conjunctions in our late anthropocene

Lord, if my dreams
        have holes.
If you still mean

for them to be holy.
        If you will
forgive me

my distractions, Lord.
        If I follow all the rules
as best as I can.

If I get caught again
        by traps set by beauty.
If beauty be the feast

of twigs my dog finds
        on our morning walk,
the photo shoots I imagine

my neighbors walk in
        and out of all day.
If they are all glittered

and bronzed
        in the purple light
of a Los Angeles dusk.

If in the city's frame
          proximate humans
call up in me a craving

to press my cheek
          on the ground.
If I want to ask

a rained on earth a secret.
          Lord, if you forgive
my desire

to be singular
          and whole,
without holes.

If it's summer.
          If not even
a single leaf

sways out of sync.
          If water is memory.
If we are scorching

the sweet earth, Lord.
          If we call that beauty.
If there's more to do

than practice looking at the sun.

MAC MESTAYER

An Incident at Cape Charles

Geologists tell us that 35 million years ago a large meteor cracked the Chesapeake Bay floor, causing mass extinctions. The epicenter was at Cape Charles, Va.

The leaves fluttered at the forest edge
    as they do today.
Shadow patterns shifted over gray trunks,
    trees rose from the soil.

Chatter and trill broke the morning sleep,
    rustle and leaf-crunch,
the thrill of sudden quiet, a squawk cut the air,
    the fog lifted her veil.

A deadly hiss, ominous roar,
    an awful cloud split the sky,
in the noise all else was quiet;
    a grand exit for billions of lives.

Again today the leaves chatter mindlessly,
    but numberless eons past
an errant star gashed the earth,
    an incident at Cape Charles.

LEE ANN RORIPAUGH

#sandhillcranes #string of beads

sizzle of orange :: lightning / the corrugated :: tin blind a gaunt bell
clanging in the wind and rain :: curious deer near to see

~

roosting overnight :: in clusters on the river's :: sandbars / cranes stirred to
call and response by the storm :: say hello (hello) hell-oh

~

scribbled warble of :: cranes graffiti night's water :: a river otter's
sleek whiskered head interrupts :: the river's tense murmuring

~

train whistle's blurred smear :: curlicued by coyotes' yip and wail ::
    the wood-block chortling
of cranes gets frenetic / as :: sun's wobbly gold yolk slides up

~

thousands of sandhills :: helix off sandbars into :: spirographed kettling
football stadium loud / iced :: river exhales puffs of fog

~

a whooping crane takes :: wing from the cornfield in snow :: ukiyo-e
cranes in snow / moon craning :: the river trills all night long

~

obfuscatory :: crooning slices through the mist :: filaments of cranes
unraveling / shaggy yarn :: from a woolly skein of fog

~

a flyover plane :: cranes burble silver water :: chirping lotto balls
oil empire's blinking neon :: signage strobes the horizon

MELINDA KOYANIS

Two Poems

Snow Blossoms

Mid-April flurries
Is it blossoms or snowflakes
Strange times it is both

Acorn Fall

First acorn
Fall
altered world
season changes
without regard

BRADLEY ALLF

Two by Two Degrees

The Big Man at Kitty Hawk sprays over the intercom: *I have*
a big plane. Big. It's a big plane and it's perfect.

The tarpaulin flexes against the aluminum while the hazard flags
keel over on the beach. *Trust me, I'm going to be your pilot,*
he rattles, *you*

love me. My father was a pilot, I have
a natural instinct for it. I know more about flying
than Orville Redenbacher.

Sand cliffs tumble into surf up and down
Jockey's Ridge and eyes of all manner of dune creatures
in the queue go wide.

The engine coughs bicycle wheels into motion
as the haggard menagerie take their seats. Two hounds
can't take the diesel fumes and whine at the lever
in the exit row.

Padding past the bulkhead, the Big Man muses *why*
would you want to get off my big, beautiful plane?

At the captain's chair he has eyes only
for the red lever. He cranks us all aloft, thirty, fifty,
three hundred cubits.

A bush baby clutches his rosary as the craft
rises into thunderheads and immediately
some among us start to drop.

The salamanders holding hands in the aisle careen
through the window, two tigers and a crab and I swear
I saw a flying fish plummet through the floorboards.

Two dials start to smoke and the Big Man grabs
a branch off the olive tree in coach to beat against
the dashboard. Sweat builds on his brow,

makes broken rainbows on the shattered glass
and the Big Man at Kitty Hawk wheezes into the intercom: *Boy
it's hot in here, how do you turn on the A/C?*

ANNA SIMS BARTEL

When we tell the story

Of how we survived the great collapse
it won't be only kindness
or sacrifice
or banning single-use plastics.

It will be imagination.
It will be flock and lift,
pull each other
up from what's broken.

Systems in collapse
don't stop collapsing.

No one can stomach the loss
of what must be lost
and so we hasten collapse
clinging to systems too heavy to hold.

We wrestle with Capital's tooth and claw,
our own creation turned against us,
all the while anchored to ground
soaked in blood.

Consider the gulls
who soar on vast wings,
dipping down to feed
taking only what they need.

Birds adapt over time
to what is real.
We are now the ostrich,
knees bent backward, running

Always earth-bound.
Afraid,
we bury our head.
But all creatures can evolve.

This is our invitation.
When we tell the story
of how we survived the collapse,
we might say:

like birds, we learned
to move as one.
We grew lighter
And lengthened our wings.

Here be dragons, cetaceans, pink crustaceans, dear humans & a book of remembrance

The cavalry's here,

loud as thunder, wild and wiser,

like a nobility

of beasts—catch the light

where x marks the spot

and if anyone asks,

this poem is a map

that lapses daily,

sees clearly two seadragons

spinning snout-to-snout

and pods of cetaceans

fueled by clouds

of pink crustaceans—

the shape of the Arctic

is less solid now,

fading into swaths

of milky blue—

and above us, dying stars

consuming their weight

in gas and dust—we're a throbbing

mass of grief and limbs

like whale food, or swollen

coastlines—do me a kindness

and repeat this worship
of humans, their book
of remembrance
a cadence of heartbeats
more than a thousand
a minute, short-winged
and foraging for flowers
which bloomed much earlier.
If I could I would
gather this shimmer—
this wonder of stars,
stop the world from burning,
the seas from rising—
be the cavalry
or a reliance of stewards:
remember what it means to love you

ANNETTE BOUSHEY HOLLAND

On the Edge

In my dream we sail upstream
to an inland lake, where
bright fish leap, and fir trees
stand in a perfect circle.

You kiss my ear and I turn
drawn to your warmth in the cold.
At some ragged edge a chainsaw
whines like a savage bug.

The whining stops.
Then comes the crack
and thud.
Echoes that ripple.

Above our floating bed
planks of pine on the ceiling
knotholes arranged like a score
diminuendo, crescendo,
finale.

We hold still, listen to
nothing. No forest is falling
no atmosphere thinning
no life disappearing.

It starts up again
a mosquito that won't go away.
Your heart beats hard beneath

my head on your chest,
and so does mine.

Conundrum

My friend says he would like to die
       and I think of that darkness, the bite

of its wind, the isolation. I don't know
       how we continue day after day

with the trees drying and burning,
       seawater filling the streets, lifting cars

to eddy them far from home, catfish
       skimming the kitchen linoleum.

The unreality of it and inescapable.
       Like watching a clichéd dystopian film

until it's your own car, your kitchen,
       your roof aflame.

                But then Autumn,

the blazing leaves, the Sandhill cranes
       overhead come down from Saskatchewan

as they have done for a thousand years,
       their gurgling calls, the flags

of their wings beating time with each other
       a fierce unmistakable joy.

SONY TON-AIME

To Be Young on The Eve of the Bois Caiman Ceremony

Fatiman, come and see.

The last mapou has fallen.

The last giant is conquered.

They have done it, zanmi m.

Their small hands have crushed life.

Look at us in the TV,

the angles of our feet,

our extended bellies.

Look into the camera, tifi.

All around us, all our eyes can see

are sugar canes and white spires;

man-made pillars of life.

Behold! The same hands that broke our backs

have come for the earth.

Vini m di w.

Look how much care and

attention they put into slicing open

the land and carving the map.

Look here, the zigzag line

that follows up north ends in darkness.

Fatiman dear, why are your hands red?

EVA CHEN

in bakers beach (love at the end of everything)

it is may again,

and everything becomes a new type of tender.

we are tethering at the edge of summer,

our youth golden & our skins raw, like mango flesh.

i watch you stare intensely into the coral blue of the ocean

feet planted into soft bodies of sand, rolling over,

you tell me that the world is ending.

corals left tooth-white & boneless by climate change.

glaciers melting like candle wax into the fade of every winter horizon.

still, nothing here has changed.

above us, looper moths circle the sky, spiraling

in perfect halos. they falter under the moonlight,

wings flinting between aluminum and copper gold.

a plover lands on the neck of a tree.

the branch buckles under its weight.

for miles around us, there is nothing but

sage bushes & memories left by half-moon lovers.

maybe we are searching for something to give our names to.

maybe we believe that if we wait long enough,

an answer will appear, washing up softly with the waves.

maybe the reason i look at you, now, is because i half expect

to find that answer, or some version of it, at least.

you laugh, and your laughter quivers in the air

like echolocation. it transforms into something sweet,

taking flight in the shape of an angel-winged tern.

i consider catching it for a moment, to cup it gently in the crease
of my hands like i do with all things i'm too afraid to lose.
instead, it slips away, & withers with the sounds
of trembling cicadas.
if we stay here too long, we will erode with the mountains.
become nothing but the fossils we find, old & bruising.

Up for Air

I.
November turns its
thoughts to spring.

Bare-armed, we walk
through late Virginia fall

beneath leaves the trees
see no need to release yet.

Out of season, dandelions
throw open their soft yellow mouths.

In the growing heat,
there is no sound.

II.
Fog over the river.
Winter evaporates.

III.
Stephen says that sea rise
won't reach our homes

even at the worst projections.
I imagine a closer shoreline,

what will be swallowed
and what can swim.

IV.
Among the waves, whales
were not plotting

an incursion.
Nothing in the sea

longed to claim
what was ours—

single family homes,
parked cars,

above-ground pools,
unkempt garden beds.

V.
No gods were left
but us, and our machines

released an unholy flood
of our own making.

VI.
Perhaps, in the deepened water,
a whale will float above our ruins,

call a name into the depths,
come up for air.

NGOC PHAM

Apocalypse with Nymph and Heirloom Tomatoes

Gripping roots with one hand, the other / clutching an empty
Tupperware, you descend / the ravine. Yesterday it stormed / and
the riverbank slips beneath you / slick as a sinkhole. This is your life
now. / EJ said there's a difference between / a *relationship* with
nature and a *connection*, / passed the joint. So you try to *connect*. /
City baby through and through, you pretend / to be the kind who
traps / spiders with a jar and piece of paper / to release them
outside, let them play / their part in the ecosystem. You pretend /
you didn't spend your childhood shooting / rats with a BB gun,
stepping on roaches / with bare feet. Didn't feel some kind of sick /
marvel when the chicken's throat twitched / against your wrist as
you held it for your father / to bleed before New Year's Eve. You
eat / vegetarian now, plant variegated tomatoes, / compost kitchen
scraps, pretend the smell / doesn't bother you as Minnesota July
heat / bakes the shit outside your bedroom window. / Graft yourself
a green thumb. Preserve / chokecherries and juneberries foraged /
from the side of the highway, greet coworkers with / "Boy we sure
needed that rain." / You let nightshade invade your garden /
because they're all part of the Solanaceae family, / tomatoes potatoes
peppers eggplants, / because *save the bees*, the wasps and ants and
hoverflies, / because Colony Collapse Disorder, shrinking glaciers, /
and that caterpillar will turn into a monarch soon, / and what are
you going to do / to stop their mass extinction?

Yesterday

an etymologist at work handed you a nymph / from the Mississippi

and you held the jar / like it contained apocalypse prophecies /

you've been tasked with decoding. Like if you kept / something alive

long enough you'd finally know / how to stay alive long enough to

witness / the end of climate change. / Indicators of pollution,

dragonfly nymphs / often die during the years it takes / to

metamorphose. You stare into the twin crystal balls / of its

compound eyes, each one flickering / with new worst-case-scenarios.

In one, your childhood / home tumbles into the river with the

trembling / resignation of a drunk. In another, bees / combust

midair. Faulty grenades. / So this is your life. You go down the

Mississippi / to fetch freshwater for your nymph. / The whole time

you fumble for foothold, / you think about your mother, half your

age, / yoking buckets of water for miles / on her bony shoulders,

haggling for another / scoop of mealworm-infested rice / with the

family's vouchers. As you stir the mud / with a twig to find tadpoles

and wrigglers, / it rains. Someone canoes by, asks / *Everything okay*

ma'am? Do you need any help? / and you squint, wipe your forehead

sweat / with dirty hand. Smile back at him all teeth. *No / I don't need*

any help. Everything is going just fine.

EILEEN R. TABIOS

Black Salted Earth

—after visiting the home destroyed during California's wildfires

You return to the opposite
of home. Fresh grass never
grew back. The universe must
have tilted as you walk on
night even as the clock confirms
noon. The scientist you hired
observed the land contained
"levels of brominated dioxins
higher than at the burning site
for electronic waste in Ghana."
You return for family left
behind: a buck, a doe, and
a fawn. You grew up with
the parents and considered
their baby your niece. You
spot only one—the father
who looks different from
the sibling in your memory.
His tail tucks tightly against
his rump, his hair stands on
end, and his ears have folded
to drop. His eyes no longer
mirror suns. You bow from

your waist to apologize—you
represent the human species.
Bowing, your gaze nears a terrain
of crushed char. You refuse to
breathe, but hiccup when you
realize animals have no choice.
When you raise your face
to look at the ruminant
you once hailed cheerfully
as "Brother!" you discover
his departure. You look
around but your eyes only
snag more ebony patches
of burnt soil. The view
matches a bleak silence bereft
of even the chirps of once-
garrulous cicadas. When
you open your mouth to
call out, you are cowed
by the introduction of a
new flavor: anguish tastes
salty. A teardrop plummets
between your lips to hijack
your tongue as the landscape
reminds you that too much
salt damages the heart.

ELLEN SANDER

Circle of Narrows

I.   A spherical aquarium with stars looking in. They know we are
     made of their destruction.

II. The similarity between the shape of the atom and that of the
     solar system transformed my childhood. I was seven. I'm still
     spinning.

III. Galileo, forced to repent his findings, was arrested anyway. He
     notated music of invisible spheres. His father was a music
     theorist.

IV. Across the Atlantic, they cut a new continent down. To conquer,
     to build, to eat and to copulate.

V.   The aquarium's sand dimpled and shifted. Grounded starfish,
     severed by tools, grew new legs.

VI. The spherical aquarium is as a balloon. As is. Pressed on one
     side, it bulges out the other. We return to a dream of deep water.

VII. The depth is in the water we avoid. We act as if nothing watches.

MARY FITZPATRICK

Atmospheric Disruption

~ honor to Brenda Hillman

Terrified I nonetheless enjoy
our extended Spring: rain and cumuli
hanging onto the San Gabriels
deep into May.
              Don't deny
we love this drought reprieve
but what price will we pay?
              Tornadoes churn
up the flat middle of this vast nation
because a massive melt
hit the arctic early. Tractors halt.
Crops soaked. Baby birds
hail-pummeled as they learn to fly.
And when sun does emerge,
shimmers with its heat.
              Almond blooms
dislodged and later, smaller
fires. The dove
who, losing her baby, tries
to build another nest
              is too late.

And I must love the floating hawk
who tells her so.

DAVID S. MADULI

Heterosigma akashiwo

Stolen sun ghostrides into the bay and detonates, wildfire's jackpot, lava's testimony, volcanic rust, estuary of napalm, Hell's marina, Lake Merritt's shore is metallic, upon closer look mounds of dead fish like fallen leaves from a silver tree, OPD chief says ShotSpotter activated, officers dispatched to the scene, multiple vehicles collision, shell casings, wastewater effluent, warmer temperatures a factor, bicyclist struck as one car fled, striped bass, sturgeon, smelt, driver, passenger, biker, harmful algal bloom, multiple gunshot wounds, pronounced dead, cascade of choke, six homicides in four days, low dissolved oxygen, underlying causes, red tide, red tide, red tide.

HEIDI MORDHOST

PROMPT: Write a Climate Crisis Poem

Richmond VA, 1980

Well, this one's right up my weed-broken concrete alley,
the milkweed twining over Mrs. May's fence,
the pokeweed dangling its gorgeous poison ink
over Dad's resolute patch of kale, the mimosa tree
pinkly tickling the roof of the shed;
the alley where we parked our two family cars,
the alley behind the yard, behind the house,
behind the four-lane divided Laburnum Avenue
that carried unsuspecting gas-guzzlers
and their passengers, citizens of the Nation of
Power and Progress, driving driving driving
over the paved lands of the Powhatan Nation.

There were bikes in the shed for fun, for riding
to the pool, for delivering the News-Leader
every afternoon, for riding to lifeguard jobs,
to hot-dog cart jobs, temporary situations until we
reached the pinnacle of maturity and could drive,
could gingerly reverse Mom's Volvo into the alley,
bump along the weed-broken concrete, edge out
onto Newport Drive and immediately collide
with a red Chrysler LeBaron. No one was hurt,
and no one learned a single lesson that could have
saved us from this gas-powered exhaust of emergency.

AMAN RAHMAN

In the Eye of the Hurricane

Broken branches lay tenderly on the soaked Earth
and on the asphalt covered by the shards of plastic
chairs. We open our door to the brief stillness, the
uneasy warmth, the streaks of sunlight, temporary.
My father calls it a cyclone. My mother, a miracle.
Storm, we name you Noah, tragedy, unforeseeable.
A candle wick burns above a puddle of melted wax
and the room is filled with honeysuckle, until it isn't.

E.W.I. JOHNSON

Collecting beach glass
along Lake Michigan, October

I hunt wave-polished glass
as the Earth sweats
salt. A blush

along dunes, trees:
each falling leaf a tally
of vanishing bees.

Beneath my feet, glimmers
buried under colonies of septarian
brown and basalt stone. Logs

rot, slimy in the lake, the loss
of memory: pine hollows, burnished
moss, bitterns banished from drained marsh.

Spun sand tears
across my face, I finger
a shard of plastic disguised as glass

and toss it. When
rusted pipes sludge
poison from steel factories,

the water blooms orange. How
much can one person do?
The unnatural calm, blue

glints between quartz,
sun caught in broken foam.
I reach down, feel

the pulse.

DAVE BONTA

Father Roach

bearer of crumbs
wielder of small wisdom

what grimy corners have
you not colonized

teaching us to focus
our loathing on you

ancestor of the boot
the settler's true spirit animal

enlarging your dominion
over all filth and squalor

thriving in ruins
weathering extremes

even able to make do
without a head

our insect father
is it you we hear

through every glory hole
and confessional

praying in a whisper
for the world
to end

CASSANDRA BOUSQUET

Dear human at the edge of time,

It is even worse than they say. Do you remember that day?
Orange sky, like a bright tangerine. It's not a cliché because this isn't
    something you ever thought would happen
President Obama had said years ago: the sun will come up in
    the morning.
Republican or Democrat, the sun will come up in the morning.
And it didn't. Darkness. Heavy with fear.
"Someday we will be with our friends again," said the Queen.
You didn't know what to believe. You were too tired for tears.

Dear human at the edge of time,
When the sky rained ash, what music were you listening to?
What book did you read when wildfires ravaged and a woman let
    seven families and a bunch of chickens in her house?
"Brown is the new green"
"Reduce, reuse, recycle"
It is a vicious cycle
False promises flicker in our eyes and die
We burn bright and angry and orange like the sky

Dear human at the edge of time,
The edge is not the end. We still have time to try.

II.

Siple Dome

After three years of drilling, we reached
bedrock, two-thirds of a mile under
the humpbacked bulge of winter.
Each season, six fresh inches of ice

put us closer to Jesus on one side,
machinery to whatever else on the other.
Sometimes the scientists gave us trash
chips to splash in our gin & tonics—

you could hear bubbles of air & ash,
dust that's fifty thousand years old crack
& pop. There's so much pressure at bottom,
it squeezes a whole century into an inch-

thick wafer of time. Neanderthals roamed
Europe. Homo sapiens still hadn't left
African plains when that sliver of core
was last exposed to the pale, thin light.

Now pieces break off the Antarctic cap
at rapid rates & float out to sea. Coastal
cities could be swamped in just a few
centuries. Sure I was drunk, but one

afternoon after work had stopped, wind
sliced through the rigging, & I'd swear
I heard singing. It was the last day
before the end of what passes for summer.

We'd soon leave for home. I spit a nickel
I'd kept warm in my mouth down the shaft
& wished. With every hole that's opened,
we fill, or hope something will come out of it.

EVERETT CRUZ

Which Ice Melts Faster?

The ones in our whiskey
or the ones at the poles? At the polls, we vote
to fix it, and when nobody does, they say to try

again. So, we scream because nobody tries,
and they tell us to vote again. We don't think
they want to try. Again. They want us to think

they'll try. They want us to chill, but the ice
is melting and flooding as the temperature rises.
We raise a glass to the world, but in our whiskey,

the ice is melting. Disappearing like hope leaving
Pandora's box, like hope leaving every ballot box.
Nothing gets fixed. We're neutered as we wait. We feel

the weight of the world like Atlas. Staring at maps,
wondering what will be underwater, we're wet
from sweat. We swear. We scream. They tell us

to vote, again, because they want us to be cool.
But the temperature rises, and our fires are burning.
Which ice melts faster? Again. Which ice melts faster?

JEREMY S. HOFFMAN

Paleoclimate Haiku

holiday music

the songs "white christmas"
and "baby it's cold outside"
might confuse my niece

paleoclimatology

if you look closely
the Earth writes vivid stories
with ice, mud, and rock

PETM carbon

humans are wily.
we emit carbon faster
than the ancient Earth.

climate proxies

like mute temple scribes
in Earth's cryptic languages
they pen climates past

attribution

we spot fingerprints
of humans loading the dice
for extreme weather

age models

one centimeter
does it capture a decade
or millennia

oxygen isotopes

the light one moves fast
the heavier one moves slow
the science of mass

foraminifera

Your calcite lattice
affected by the ocean
is the Earth's yearbook

LEE ANNE GALLAWAY-MITCHELL

Ogallala Aquifer

Preacher says *Your dad had*
the best water in the county.
That's a hell of a thing to say

To farmer's daughters. And then
To follow it with a farmer's regret:
He should have spent more time

With his girls. His regret: the time,
Not a legacy of daughters, no sons.
He loved his family, his country,

And Lockney, Texas. (His salvation,
His damnation.) All that nation
Of fortunate sons, their condemnation.

He sold the farm before he bought it.
He crushed the can before he kicked it,
Drinking less because his kidneys told

On him, said take this job and shove it.
After one of the half a dozen times
He almost died that year, I tell my dad

About the cienegas here in Arizona,
How I go looking for these wetlands
In miniature, how like playas from home.

When I tell him of the cienagas, he talks
About cleaning out an old well for new use
On his land (no longer his) once. He said:

You'll never run out of water here, figuring
Water as infinite as nothing like time.
As a taken for granted creek now vanished

We knew better the names of what didn't
Belong (like our own), of the weeds we had
To kill, not the plants that we could grow.

CLAIRE WAHMANHOLM

P

P is for picture book, the pillow at our backs, my daughter in her Peppa Pig pajamas. P is for peace and peace lily and Peace rose; for *peek-a-boo* and *this little piggy*. I open *Plip-Plop Pond*'s flashspun polyethylene pages and point to the polliwogs and lily pads. Let P not be for the Permian Basin and its pipelines and petrochemical plants. Let the phosphorus not proliferate, the pH not plunge. I flip to Paddington, perched politely outside the Lost Property Office, and try not to picture the cruise ships pumping sewage into Peruvian ports. But P is for plague ship. P is for Point Nemo, where de-programmed spacecraft pinwheel into smaller and smaller rain, pepper the waves with paint chips. Around it, the Garbage Patch purls its plastics into pieces smaller than plum pits, smaller than pixels, pinpricks, plankton. P is for plastic, more permanent than permafrost. I open *Each Peach Pear Plum* to spy it hidden in the ptarmigan, the pheasant, in the phthalo blue of the Portuguese man o' war. I read *The Princess and the Pea* and feel the pellets in each layer of the ocean: epipelagic, mesopelagic, past where light penetrates, into the bathypelagic, abyssopelagic, where scientists have found polyester in the molten putty between the Pacific and Philippine plates. P is for the pontoons of Polar Spring, Propel, and Panama Blue. I sing "Baby Beluga" and see pods of pilot whales with pool floaties pretzeled inside their pelvic cavities. I turn the page but it's a palindrome of panic. The petrel preens petroleum from its plumage. The propeller pulps the back of the porpoise. The pressure on my windpipe will not unwrap itself. My daughter has slipped into sleep. I place her outside my arm's parenthesis so she can't feel my pulse pounding. *P is for parachute*, I whisper. *P is for pearl, penicillin, picnic, planetarium, platypus, plink, the pocket-sized pipistrelle, the Ponderosa and its pine beetles.* I turn up the pink noise on her sound machine so she can't hear that P is also the end of *chirp, tulip, kelp, scallop, icecap, sleep.*

JEANINE PFEIFFER

Precipitate

screech, squawk, go the rusty hinges of the steel back door
thwap as it bangs open
       and I am surprised — shocked, even —
       at the wetness staining our Oakland deck,
       dampening my dog's paws
       on her morning foray into the grass.

We are being kissed by rain
       (and that's what it is — a mere kiss, *un besito*—)
       our lands mired in the drought of a millennium
       ("1200 years" say scientists, with dry precision)

Our intimacy with this drought is magnified daily:
my lips, unkissed,
have lost their wetlands, their bird song —

a personal climate change

Counterposed against a warming planet
where I grow colder,
the passages to my heart's rivers constricted
       by fragmented icebergs, precipitous ice floes
       providing inadequate refuge
       to the blood-smeared mother bear
       raging across my tundra

We choose, and choose, and choose again:
always a matter of degrees —

the 180-degree pivot   (or not)
the 2-degree tipping point   (or not)

We embrace want
we drown in the dry

An anthropogenic agony,
dust unto dust,
prematurely.

Who is willing to forfeit their carbon?
To reclaim, redouble, once hoarded oxygen?

Who will release their tightly cupped hands
allowing the ultimate blessing to flow
into the cracks and fissures of a world
        where separation has become our unspoken language
        inscribed with unshed tears
        onto a collective parchment.

AMANDA M. BLAKE

Displaced

displaced
is a nice word
for refugee
where my home
which once was here
a pin on a map
a series of numbers
that told letters
where to go
is now there
and no one knows
what to do with it now
because it's upside-down
and half filled with
solidified mud
on another's land
halfway through
another's house
almost like
possession
which is nine-tenths
of the law
but we are strangers
who didn't sign up
to share

and i'm pretty sure
someone else
was in there
and now isn't
but who can tell
in the overlap
who owns
those bones
how suddenly
homes strewn
mark a world's ruin

ALLEN BRADEN

Habituation

Whenever fishermen encircle

    the circle

they bring whiskey, buck knives,

    cold

They taste a dream of pike, its

    smoky

It's been said fish hunker

    low

dim. Schools lose all sense of

    direction.

and bitch about the twitch taking

    root

In the glow of the television's

    new

in long johns, reliving the

    urge

To the lake these men return,

    without

without knowing anything but

    instinct.

sawn through the layers of winter,

cuts, jerky, snus and folding chairs.

meat luring them again to Skookum Lake.

through the season until numbed days

Mornings the wives meet for coffee

at the base of their husbands' spines.

year, their men doze and wriggle

to cross bedsheets of January ice.

knowing why; pike resurface,

KRISTIN BERKEY-ABBOTT

Higher Ground

On the last day of the year, Noah's wife waits
for the insurance adjuster.
She thinks of the Christmas flood
and the larger flood before it.

Her husband's god speaks
in terms of measurements and building
instructions. Her husband's god gives
out directions and punishments.

Noah's wife has always heard
the subtle messages, the daily
communications that the men
ignore: how to feed
the family, how to comfort
the forsaken, which breaches
need repairing.

Noah's wife studies
real estate listings and elevation charts
while she waits
for the insurance adjuster.
She should be researching
vehicles. She already knows
what the adjuster will tell
her about the drowned car.
She seeks answers
to the larger question
of how to find
the higher ground.

JOSHUA MCPEAK

Beached

I sit beside the satin sea and see a beached whale whining in an unmoored voice. A moonbeam falls on dying blubber. Plastic spills from its maw. A thousand locust crabs crawl up an ink-black tail that sent it bounding through the oceans once, a thing unbound from weight and oil. But that was many years ago. I watch it die and croon on a deathbed of dunes, unsure of what to do. If I roll it off that sunless shore, will it once more sing hymns and swim its swim of kings? It sings a song I know too well. An elegy to weightlessness. An ode to where it once could go. But that was many years ago, and the years ahead are dead.

KYLE POTVIN

Ask the Children

Who will protect the porpoise?
The mollusk with its ancient shell?

> Women gather on the beach to prepare,
> toughening muscled arms.

Who will guard the gulls, and the pelican
plunging with its empty pouch?

> Maybe this woman knows.

She swims in the chilly sea
floating foam and salt to shore.

> Or this one who inspects seaweed
> and soft bird bones. Rubs them

between her fingers like soap.
What is that cry?

> Oh, infant mewling, toddler fussing,
> Tell us: What should we do?

Child, when you were small you told me something
impossible was going to happen. And it did.

RAJIV MOHABIR

From Whalelore

Oahu, 2022

Once I saw a whale spout from Waimānalo though it is rare
because it is protected by a reef—or a fallen volcano whose mouth
extended from Waimānalo to Kailua to the Nuʻuanu Pali. In a ten-
minute gathering I was able to find a Gerber jar full of plastics—
most no bigger than my pinky fingernail—in one place as I sat
down in the sand.

Individuals are not the culprits—our choices matter of course but
not as much as the pollution allowances of governments the world
over and especially in the US, known for being the most wanton
insatiable consumers, allowing corporations to devastate the earth
and its resources for capitalist gain. Land, air, sea, space, this country
wants to own it all in its failed modernist project of national identity.
America, America.

Even though the humpbacks are opportunistic feeders in the
Hawaiian waters, they do eat here by lunging after sparkling schools
and shoals. Their feeding patterns, outside of theirs Hawaii-fast,
includes group and cooperative feeding in the Alaskan waters using
bubble nets and belly flashes where the Subpolar Gyre clouds the
water amidst the algal blooms and capelin and sardine shoals. As
they lunge with their mouths open, their throats' ventral pleats
expand, and they are capable of taking in five thousand gallons of
water that they push out through their baleen—made of keratin
hanging from their upper pallates. The frayed baleen functions as a
filter to catch all the prey species for humpback. Using their tongues,
they guide their food towards their grapefruit sized throats.

When they lunge into clouds of fish, their impressive jaws also
engulf countless plastic shards, which they then swallow as a result of
it being mixed with their food. From this, plastics enter the whale
biome. As we all know, or if you don't shame on you, that plastics
never biodegrade. They break down and poison us.

Some plastics for medical reasons actually help aid human life. I am
dependent on plastics for my medicines for diabetes, without which
and without whose waste, my life would most likely be considerably
shorter. At Waimānalo Beach–Sherwoods I went walking from the
entry gate through the wooded area. The beach water gleamed
opalescent as I approached.

Amalia and I put down our things and set up our sunning and shade
spots. As we sat there, I started to gather little bits of plastic from the
sand. The pieces were shard like, pitted from floating in the surf.

> They call the new element
> of plastic melted onto rock
> a plastiglomerate–
>
> a new substance of the Anthropocene.
>
> But what of our biological
> constitutions? Are we new beings,
> bioplastiglomerates, made partially
> of plastic, filled with it?

From Whalelore

Oahu, 2022

The poet Stephen Collis visited UH when I was a student there and in his reading in the Korean Studies building told us that humpback whales swallow six times more plastic than fish as they feed the Pacific.

I thought about how much plastic there is in the food chain. In our fish, breast milk, in our organs that we just can't even imagine as yet —the injurious and cancerous effects stalking us.

I remember how there were accounts of sperm whales being pulled up from the beach and sheets upon sheets of plastic masquerading as giant squid filled their bellies until they starved from being so crammed with the indigestible polychlorides there was no room for anything else.

There are three great garbage gyres in the pacific swirls from Asia to the continental US and south guided by the currents:

In the arctic there is the Subpolar Gyre guided by the North Pacific, Alaska, Kamchatka, and Oyashio Currents.

Below that in the North Pacific the gyre is formed by the motion of the North Equatorial, Kuroshio, California, and North Pacific currents.

The South Pacific Gyre is born of the movements of the East Australia, the South Equatorial, Peru, and Antarctic Circumpolar currents.

These are objects found swirling in the Great Pacific Garbage Patch

        Lighters, rainbows of bottle
        caps, toothbrushes: pink and green,
        milk jug rings, fragments fingernail-sized.

        Tarps, frayed shower liners:
        a confetti, bags for coffee and Peek Freans,
        shards of twist offs and bottle

        necks. buckets flakes, tackle, tires,
        old rope and fork tines gleam
        fragmenting, fingernail-sized.

        Solo cups and spoons, swirls gyre
        of toothpicks, smashed figurines,
        "reduced plastic" water bottles,

        discarded netting, who knows what, a mire
        of broken toys, a dazzling sea-cloud
        of fragments the size of a fingernail.

        Ziplocs, iPod cases, spice jars, dire
        razor sharp calculator face shards teem,
        swirling there, prescription pill bottles
        in siennas, the size of your fingernail.

AIMEE NEZHUKUMATATHIL

Triggerfish Invective

The last time I sank my face in the neritic ocean
I found only beige and bleached out bones, not orange

and green coral fans. I spoke to angry underwater
ghosts in other languages I forgot I knew—full

of seaweed syllables and cracked shells.
Too many pale bodies have marched

their plastic fins over this coral, taking selfies
on the coral, scrubbing coral clean of leafy food.

Not even leaving a scintilla of small-shelled
meats. The ghosts answer with a cackle and hiss

and light-scatter. The sea in this bay once curved
full of cucumbers and other funny vegetables, some

with fin and some with spine. Here the sea
like a swollen ring of motion burst—here the sea

throws a dozen fish with a pointed snout towards
me. I never thought I'd see triggerfish in real life

but here they are–almost a warning or last chance.
Why else would they activate their trigger fin

and hold on to coral bones with no more promise?
I am certain I will gain an anklet of tiny bites

from these humuhumunukunukuapua'a and why not:
for all the fish I see now, there were thousands

more just last year. And the last year. And the last.
The underwater ghosts only send out mondegreens.

Some scattered pale green light. A cackle and hiss.

CLAIRE MILLIKIN

Summerweight

Some blankets and jackets advertise *summer weight!*
as if that could ease what's lost,
the shoulders of a thousand tons of ice

melting into oceans, gathering heat like grief.
We'd smoke at the open window, summer's weight bending
live oaks in damp heat, workers out of breath.

The hard work of my childhood was learning not to disappear,
hiding by backyard trash cans until my mother stepped outdoors
late in the weight of sultry August light, walking

beyond willows to throw away the refuse after supper.
I wanted nothing but to continue existing
as a form of love, waiting by the family trash cans

to see her face, to see her finally see me
after the long hot day. Thick with salt witness
the weather becomes our bodies.

The day's belting heat fills with precarious species,
voiceless or almost unvoiced animals.
Refugia, a crossroads to the future.

SOFIA FALL

Spill

To Line 5

Even when the Earth was warmer there was still water
in Michigan. It was years and years ago—an age of jawed
and bony fish and vanished glaciers. The Silurian.
In elementary school I did not understand that the name

reached impossibly backwards into time. What I learned
was close and simpler: before, there was a warm,
shallow sea. I had never been to the ocean. I could not
imagine anything except the freshwater horizon

I'd been born to. I dreamed of water that burned
your lungs, water you could not drink, a world
below the surface you could not open your eyes to.
It horrified me more than drowning. I was afraid

it might come flooding back one morning by surprise.
It was not the water I was scared of but the spill
of salt into the Lakes like poison. My mother
tried to teach me my mistake. The sea left

fossil corals turned to stone that churn within the Lakes
in Michigan. If you walk the shoreline you can find one,
and we did. I curled my fingers around it, failed
to fully imagine a time before the glaciers melted

into Great Lakes, although I knew there was evidence,
although I was holding it in my hands. I threw the stone

away into the water, willed it to be eaten by the waves.
I only loved this world. I did not want any other.

Is it wrong to say I'm still afraid of the spill of time,
how heat eats up the order of the atmosphere and the poisons
of past worlds are melted into this one? I love
the Great Lakes. I love their fish and birds

with hollow bones. There is no other time
in which they will be found as stone. They are creatures
of this water. I only love this world.

O Human

o human

o further

o communities
o prosperity

o continue o damage

North

north

North

northeast

Niño
Northern

o cause   *o American*

o increasingly

o reduce

o the growing

o increasingly

worl

o occur

o cause

stress

o the

o mismatches

o sea
o be

Nuisance
National

number

o interconnected   o a range

o interconnected
o individual   o anticipate   o missed

                                                      number

        no
    no   NOAA

                        o increasingly

result   o

        o consider

        o adapt   o build

number

number   nights

                                number   nights

                                        National

Natural   National

                    o reduce
o lower
                                                    o not
        o avoid   o the economy

                                                    o decision

AUTHOR'S NOTE: I created this erasure poem by taking the 4th National Climate Assessment (NCA4) Summary Findings and the NOAA (National Oceanic and Atmospheric Administration) State Climate Summaries websites and applying The Deletionist.com to the pages. I printed and then cut-up the results into sections, rearranging the sections to create a cut-up poem. (Unused pages have been reused or recycled). "The Deletionist is a concise system for automatically producing an erasure poem from any Web page. It systematically removes text to uncover poems." It was created by Amaranth Borsuk, Jesper Juul, and Nick Montfort. "The Deletionist works to make every page into a single poem." "The Deletionist" is "neither an artificial intelligence nor a poetry generating system." Information from thedeletionist.com

November

I pick the last cherry tomatoes
from their brown, withered vines.
How have the chipmunks missed
these red globes on this frosted morning?
A handful—enough for me to pull
off my glove and pluck fruit from the branch.
I'm not a gardener, can't tell a sucker
from stem, but today after raking
the last leaves from the silver maple,
I want to honor all endings—the cycles
and seasons—with a bit of lettuce, tomato,
sunflower seeds, the drizzle of dressing
as chickadees hunt and peck beneath the feeder
tasting whatever sweetness
still remains in the world.

ANGELA NARCISO TORRES

Harvesting the Heart

In Florida, I shall eat a palm seed and see if that'll grow a new heart for me.
—D.H. Lawrence

Indeed, swallowing a seed seems the better option.
For stealing the palm's heart from its solitary stem
is back-breaking work and spells certain death
for the tree. The part you can eat, also known
as swamp cabbage, lobster of vegetables,
burglar's thigh, lies deep in the woody bark
just where the fronds start. You need a machete
to work down the trunk, stripping layer after
jagged layer, each the weight of a small child.
Some give up by the third or fourth. But near
the core the flesh is tender, drenched with sap.
You'll be surprised, despite how much bark
you've skinned—knuckles raw, fingers
splintered—the sheer size of that heart.

ERIC FORSBERGH

Outside of Denver

Is the American West in a Megadrought?
                              The Economist.

We're on the interstate, not just us, but especially
the truckers, getting buffeted by prairie wind.
To our left, a high-tension pylon crumples,
an old soldier with a heavy pack, onto parched grass.
We see smoke rise, at first like a dark creek roiling in the thaw.
Quickly then, like a file of brown horses in a rolling gallop, up, up.
Soon, a wide herd of buffalo stampeding to the sky.

The wind rakes flames across dry suburban lawns and
outruns cars pouring like ants out of cul-de-sacs.
Black-yellow smoke swallows the sun, and homes by the hundreds.
First the plastic siding bubbles, then melts and sags like a Dali painting.
Tar shingles curl and burst.
Rapidly, posts and beams define themselves in blinding orange lines.
Showers of debris cascade like streams of burning hair and
the mall goes up—nail salon, organic store, yoga studio, minute clinic—
the ever-convenient life rendered to ash.

County sheriffs ring the roads. Fire trucks converge in caravans.
Across the highway at the hospital, a scrum of ambulances waits its turn.
By night, from satellite, the necklace of fire displays
its smoke-choked loveliness. Seen from the next prairie town away,
the hotel shimmers like a gem, collapsing last.

MARY GRACE BERTULFO

Feast

Thirst hides in the small things—
piercing—
who are not *things*
but wings and striped abdomens
turned ruby red at dusk,
the drops of my blood, our bond,
as they buzz and needle.
Culex mosquitoes and our
        Bertulfo family reunion,
navigate the choking summer heat
and feed our respective broods.

Guitars serenade our backyard
        dinner-party—
moments stolen—
from clicking laptops, sanitized
        desks, and Corona isolation.
Lola Mely and Lolo Jun flew
halfway across America to meet
Baby Elias, pleasant plumpness
        and folds,
and pass him on our exuberant
bouncing knees around patio tables
piled with pancit noodles and oil-
        stained pizza boxes.

We endure—
trying not to wilt,
beaded sweat unable to evaporate.
Cousins squeal and shoot clear
        arcs of water.

I pull strips of damp blue cloth,
make-shift kerchiefs, from the fridge.
Tie frosty knots in the dimples of
        our necks.
We hold on
fifteen minutes more, an hour, four.
Who knows when we'll be
        together, again?

Tempests from whirring fan blades
confuse flying bloodsuckers.
Protective—
We swat the tender crooks of
        Baby Elias' knees
fending off fevers,
the threat of vomit,
dreading spots and splotches from
        West Nile Virus.
Hungry mosquito mamas
siphon our lifeblood.
Which of them carries the disease?

Next morning, I drain—
rain from flower pots,
puddles from dented plastic tables,
prevent hundreds of wigglers
        from hatching.
The fury of climate chaos bruises
        our calves.
Our reunion continues,
        unabated, as red welts rise.

Multitasking Log

check work email, read about flooding in Puerto Rico, put lotion
on my dry legs, Spectravite vitamin bottles on dining room table,
half-eaten bowl of granola, sip warm coffee, try to remember next
PT appointment, listen to bird songs on YouTube which makes me
think of the bird on yesterday's walk, my friend trying to ID with
an app on her phone, the announcement by Taco Bell that their
guacamole would not suffer from the impact of Mexico's dearth of
avocados, text my siblings, leg stretches, where should I donate my
clothes, picture my mother alone in bed at the monastery, the
abbess in her kuti sending out newsletters on compassion, work on
blurb for G, new sit-stand desk doesn't work, scratch the spreading
rash on torso, soldiers gun down village in Myanmar, accidentally
text to a client two close-up photos of the scars on my abdomen
which I meant to send to my doctor at Kaiser: a thin trail of blood
in one, the other shaped like a star, navel exposed, my hand
holding up my right breast.

EMILY SCHULTEN

In the Eye

The moon is a pit in your stomach
and it grows like swift cancer
in your throat. You can't see it.
You'd swear it's the most perfect day
you've ever lived in, the heron's song
as if for love is clear and reverberates
between the glassy-eyed sea and
the acrylic azure sky.
        But by the time the moon
emerges, the rumors are as swift
and as changed as the churned
ocean approaching. And it is the end.
You go for cover, create a bunker
in your bed, your windows sealed
like a coffin, the night permanent
until the gust has finished having
her way with you. You find the food
in your cabinets that is kept in jars.
You find spoons and the one radio
station that will keep talking
through the fuzz. The lights fail.
But the man's voice keeps on, repeats
the worst of it until it's safe for you
to leave your bed, blink and squint
your eyes in the sun. And then he's
the only sound there is, his static
and relief, until you walk a ways
and see a neighbor you may or may
not recognize. You limbo under

snapped and spitting wire, you
scale the uprooted sidewalk, you
dodge the shingles at your feet
and hear someone say (what a relief
to hear someone say!) you're about
to trip over the white picket impaled
in the almond tree. Nothing is
recognizable. The landscape
of your life doesn't exist anymore.
Houses, shops, docks, and graves:
they're misplaced into abstraction
or altogether gone. Occasionally,
the whir of a generator or a holler
from another end of the island.
You can't believe what you see,
          what you don't see.
You think of the moon again,
what it must feel like to step onto it.
And in this way you conjure it,
call it back to the sky
where it's the only light save
the stars that are tangible braille
in the absence of all messages.
But the moon has changed,
you don't feel it inside anymore.

MARISA LIN

cosmology of loneliness

there is a moon. there is a star. there are braids of what-ifs roping their orbits around a planet. a bear staring up at a cloud, haunches thick against thinning ice. a girl, running. eyes socketed to the part of her brain that claims the terrain is unsteady and that she is falling, collapsing like her gut caving in like endangered silk, strands unraveling in a promise evaporated. there is gravity. there are floods. there is a gaggle of nebulae straying too close to a black hole. then a popsicle, melting. mailbox, agape. mouths cursing the sun, minister of wildfires retaking prairies without apology. there is ash. atmosphere clouded over by the memory of exhausts, of production, of moving once-alive acres across oceans to be eaten. have we lost our names? there is a village that was once a village. a human that was once a home. now even asteroids find solace in orphans thrusting themselves into seas hungry for last things. like a girl, left for another. an animal, waiting for dissolution. for who said we were the marrow of everything? every spring hearts are broken, a breathing creature disappears, and the earth heats up by degrees. we leave every bone of ourselves to be parched by winds we have poisoned for profit. where is the money, they ask, and we point to this dwindling pebble of sky as the galaxy moves on, moves on, she moves on—

no thousand vernal moons
can keep our skins from drowning
these swift, swift blossoms

Someone Had Better Be Prepared For Rage

During the hurricane we came to learn
almost anything, given wind enough
and rage enough, could turn into a weapon—

our old TV antenna's bony fingers,
the neighbor's mailbox wrestled from its pole,
the solid metal door to our garage,

which buckled, broke, and blew away. Roof tiles'
machine-gun stutter pummeled and chipped the wall
we leaned against, while the beams of someone's roof

sailed through the air, knocking out window frames
and doors. Stakes and shrapnel rose from the ground
as if some angry god were hurling missiles,

or the damaged earth itself had turned on us,
yet outside the room we cowered in,
the tree we thought would kill us swayed and stood.

DIANA WOODCOCK

What It's All About

These days rampant
with a global pandemic,
it's all about keeping the dark
at bay while believing
pure faith is a ray of it.*

And though I feel isolated,
I am liberated as I take action
in language, finding connection.

These days of climate change,
it's all about walking lightly
on this earth, listening
to all who are speaking
beyond words — the elephants,
wolves and killer whales.

It's about silence and stillness,
turning off all electronic devices
to listen to and watch the breeze
rustling the leaves, to let each
fleeting moment's meeting
of insect, flower and bird
be savored and preserved.

These days of global social unrest,
it's all about trying our best
to speak the truth, to bend the arc
toward justice, to seek a zone
of peace for all sentient beings.

These days of too much death,
it's all about taking time to reflect
on what all is left, and resting
in knowing the fact that from
the center a fountain is flowing —
that with amazing grace, we can
survive this dark time and place
to arrive on higher ground.

John of the Cross

KIM SHUCK

Tilting Planet

Watch the lake dry the
Gradual crack the
Tea of things that were in the
Water we are
Water these are the
Birds we've never seen before
Play hide and seek with
Lightning all the way from
San Francisco to
Someone else's students the
Snow
Snow in June and a bloom of
Crickets on the road the
Road was crawling the world is
Miracles and maybe doesn't need us
Anymore the
Power lines in Texas
Knee deep in new ponds are we in a
Chase is this a
Chase do we know where we are
Running the dry air and the
White hilltops the
Wind howls more these days and
Some cry
Not our fault and as the water rises
How long will they cry these are our
Songs these
Rivers a
Song for the Colorado another
Bone a
Bone in the drying places

Baseline

It doesn't seem like you should be able
to hold panic like a too-full cup
all day. But all day it sloshes
and slips inside of me. Just a little.
All day I think about the glaciers.
I think about the clever invention
to sieve garbage out of the sea
and wonder where that garbage
will go. All day my children's faces
shine like exit signs at the edge
of my mind's eye. And yes,
when the world
is too much with me,
I go to the woods. But the range
of the maples is moving northward
faster than the maples can move, & the ash
trees are being eaten alive, & the winters
are too warm to kill the ticks
which infest the moose
until they lose so much blood
they do actually die of it.

I think of the dinosaurs, and the meteor,
and, strangely, sadly,
it comforts me—
how nearly everything died.
Yet here we are.

III.

LUISA A. IGLORIA

Ode to the Never-ending

The universe says you'll get smacked
    with a lesson as many times as it takes

for you to learn it—If that's so, what
    lesson could possibly be in this tiny,

annoying hair that keeps growing back
    in the same spot, on the right side of

your chin? You stand on tiptoe to get a better
    angle at the mirror; tweezers in hand, you

pull it out, marveling at how a small irritation
    commands total absorption. A week later,

it's back—nagging feeling, indeterminate itch.
    In Virginia Beach, 4 dead humpback whales

have washed up on the shore since
    the beginning of the year—you could say

they are also a kind of lesson that hasn't
    been learned. Necropsies show injuries

consistent with vessel strikes in waters
    thick with ship traffic. If the world is ending,

each cetacean body that perishes on sand
    is a fallen leaf, a wound bled open in the middle

of a horizon of false starts. We keep saying
    there's time, the window's still open. Until it's not.

JORDAN STEVEN SHER

Fade to Orange, to Gray, to Black

Is it dark where you are?

Hot, cold, wet, dry?

What have we done?

The sky is a deeply muted orange film where I am

The smoke a dusty gray veil

Disturbing the Sun

Indistinguishable from every other day

Gray like the grizzled beard I only trim when the power is on

Gray like the faded vision that visits me now

I peer out of the double-paned glass from my small home as I

imagine other fellow specters do in what once was a city, or

was it a desert, or a farm

The race I come from, human, gave up on itself long ago

There were brave ones, outspoken ones

But, alas, the monied ones won out; they always did

Or, did they?

Where are they now?

Under the same sky

Maybe

Equality finally reached

The rich, the poor, the in-between

This is what remains of Earth

Is it dark where you are?

CRAIG SANTOS PEREZ

Shall I compare thee to the anthrop'cene?

recycling Shakespeare's Sonnet 18

Shall I compare thee to the anthrop'cene?
Thou art more stable and more auspicious:
High tides do rise the level shores of Sea,
And humans' reign hath too short an epoch;
Sometime too warm the fuel of fossil shines,
And often is his great derangement bing'd;
And every fact from fact sometime denies,
By lies or media's fake news unhing'd;
But thy endless holocene shall not shroud,
Nor mass extinction of species thou ho'st;
Nor shall doom nuke thou poison'd in his cloud,
When in variant lines to clime thou gho'st:
So long as we save seeds and bees survive,
So long hopes this, and this gives hope to thrive.

CATHERINE HULSHOF DE LA PEÑA

A patch of sky so small

A patch of sky so small.
We reach beyond and fall.
Tiny scars then we colonize Mars.
I hold moon rocks and your tiny hand.

I sing you lullabies.
I buy you fireflies.
Ocean where there was land.
And then the stars become the sand.

BRIAN TURNER

Hyperion

*...the darkness they rise from is their own creation,
and high in their canopies, lichens not found below,
delicate as fog, and birds that might as well be angels.*
                                        —Robert Wrigley

The fires of 2020 have burned their epitaphs into history.
In the redwood forests of California, on the far side of winter,
snow falls in slow drifts through the ancient crowns that disappear
in mist. It is a grove of giants, with an understory of burnt madrone
and tanoak, laurel and red alder, sword fern returning with blade-shaped
chevrons of green. Roosevelt elk graze on the fresh leaves of sorrel
unfurling from stems rising through char. Pine martens hunt
among the deadfall of the younger trees and the clustered trunks
that magnified the fire's heat, much of it reduced to a crush of ash.

Overlooking it all, at 379.1 feet, Hyperion, the tallest tree on Earth.
It is six to eight hundred years old, from the genus *Sequoia sempervirens*.
I close my eyes. Breathe in the sweet perfume. A wandering salamander
rests on a matting of moss, sliding its tongue under a globe of dew
to guide it into its mouth—as if drinking a liquid portrait of the forest.

Remember the carved wheel of a redwood we once saw?
Twelve to fifteen feet in diameter, that horizontal slice was displayed
so that we could walk up and touch its raw interior, its history.
The droughts. The good times. Years of green and gold scribed
in concentric circles, with centuries of life detailed in the heartwood.
It was something like a vinyl record turned on its edge, and you said—
If we could play it somehow, imagine what we'd hear. Your fingertips
traced the grooves. And as I think of this, I hear the birdsong in the mist.
Hermit warblers. Dark-eyed juncos. Otherworldly voices feathering down.

How wistful the trees must be, and heartsore, considering us.
We are given such a brief time to love. A few years, only.
Moments. Some of it archived within the trees themselves.
The way our voices whispered as the falling snow erased
the flame-shaped leaves, dampening the cross-hatching
of mulch at our feet. The things we shared. Secrets.
The way we lifted our faces and closed our eyes
to listen. The way our fingers braided together
as we walked into the silence of the grove.

KINDRA MCDONALD

An Antidote to Our Despair

Scientists have found my daily obsession
over the bird feeder to be normal
more than that, even helpful
for grief and the dark that clouds

my thoughts like cataracts. Research
links birdwatching with improved well-being
and birdsong a reason to restore our faith
in the natural order of the world

this must be why my grandmother
always said to feed the birds before bed.
In my city we live our lives by hightide
and wetlands watch, the whim of the Army Corps

and seawalls they rename "lines of protection".
I am smack in the middle of a 100-year flood zone
nestled between the Elizabeth River and the Chesapeake Bay
and my car floats down 26th street at every full moon

summoning ship makers and sailors and I drift until
I feel like I could fly. In my paradise
everyone ambles with binoculars and notepads
a collective group of stretched necks looking up

a bingo sheet of bird achievements and the practiced
sweet-sweet song a whistled lullaby. I learn to identify
the greedy sound of the crow from the raven
the finch from the wren. Find hummingbird nests

small as thimbles and come to know that birds sing
to their incubating eggs so they will know the call
of their species before they ever hear them. I'd never
hatch. Sweet, sweet, I'm so sweet, the call

of the yellow warbler echoes in my DNA.
In the North Landing River, a place preserved and full
of rare species, stopping point for migratory songbirds
I believe in antidotes when I see that little flash

moon me in the bare branch of January thaw. As if
I clutched in my small fist a vial labeled *happy*
to swig with abandon. The warbler sings for us
flashes his golden rump, could care less if my hair

is washed, my pants too snug, my heart sluggish
and slow, and somehow the birds make me forget

the sea inching closer calling for us all.

Debris

Down the mountain, two cars
careen off the freeway
at high speed, dragging dirt
and dust, grinding to a halt
in the median. Everyone stops.
I call the cops. They know
and so the wait begins.

It's warm, so I stay out
and nod to strangers, shattered
back light plastic strewn across the wet
asphalt underfoot. It crunches
and I think about how it came
from some place invisible
to almost everyone—manufactured
via some cloaked process (outsourced
overseas). My phone informs me

one component has been stripped
down to as few minted pieces
of millimeter-thick copper-plated zinc
as is possible. And then it's shipped
in bulk and plugged into some assembly line,
inserted a few inches above a bumper
and forgotten until now
or maybe a few minutes ago
as the rear-ender glowed red
just before impact.

A tow truck driver sweeps
the shiny fragments toward the shoulder,
stepping over and on the burned
trace the tires left (black and curved).
I realize I can smell them,
a scented remnant of velocity,
paint and canvas that exist as microcosms
of each other. After an hour

we are moving again. I never pass
the second car—it never appears:
was hoisted up a flatbed, carried off,
soon to be a hay bale with hydraulics,
left to rust, and never unwrinkle,
a self-contained collision collecting
snow, soot, and dust somewhere
deep inside, the driver's DNA
dried to the now-dyed fabric,
another story for another day,
and they will tell it to their kids
when one asks about the webby scar
on that arm as they drive
in their brand-new car
past the saplings the old one
upended, still snapped in half.

She says

1.

A naturalist is a nature interpreter, she says
Almost annoyed, bothered that I do not know the obvious.
    I hear Nature needs to be interpreted by someone else
    but me.

Phragmites, those long woody reeds are invasive, she says
We tear them down again and again and it's labor-intensive.
    Invasive means Not Native, I hear. Am I invasive?

Extirpated means locally extinct, she says
It's not gone forever, it's gone form here.
    Someone is responsible for this, I hear. Is that me?

Leaves of three, leave it be, it's poison ivy, she says.
Alive or dead, the rash will mount, the leaves, the vines, even the
    smoke of it burning.
    I hear poison is Native — leave it be.

Exposure leads to allergy, she says
You may be born immune, too much in contact will transgress
    your protections.
    I hear there's no accommodation, only aggravation.

Bullfrogs will eat their own babies, she says
It's quite common in the animal reign, it's all a question of need.
    Would I eat my own baby, I hear — when in such need?

Horseshoe crabs are among the oldest living species on Earth, she says,
Scientists harvest their blood for medical research, it's an immense
     wealth of knowledge.
          Don't ever get that old! is what I hear.

Why did you want to become a naturalist, I ask.
Always felt at home outside, she says.
          Always felt at home outside, is what I too say.

KHATY XIONG

Aubade

By morning, the myth finally faded.
Whole oceans reduced to a single drop.
Lamenting throughout the landscape,
caverns and canyons, blisters of islands
seething in natal forms. The earth cornered
in every rock. By memory, the lowland deer
emerging from their graves in an attempt
to graze. Slow and thirsty, they drink
unnoticed in these fields. Their mossy flanks
dribbling with precious dew. What else
was there to do? I covered my mouth
    and bowed deeply.

In grief there is also desire—
a shiny arrow void of all purpose. My life
a paradisal canvas bursting with spells
and sores of the gilded tongue. Meteoric,
blood aglow, my shadow parting through
my bones. And for a time, everything
living for too long and not long enough.
My mother, who died quickly, tossed
hastily into the wind. My despair tumored
    and blooming, oneirically untraceable.

Beyond desire, the accursed dreams—
birds mending borderlands, beasts felling
stars, eternal life in the eye of the garden.
Upon the tides, the celestial idyll betrayed
by dark. Such is the will of a seeded colony,

the devoured home sailing into absurdity
without guide or glossary. Needletails
sending off into the sky in lieu of sacrifice.
Were I to wake from this, I would miss
my mother turning away from me, spring
inflorescent, the isle of dawn breaking
        over my left middle knuckle.

SHERI REDA

Jumpfrog

Cold slaps on again like latex, a blizzard
scours the pigeon-cote sky. Sickroom blue sheds
ashen shivers down from dirty rafters. Particulates
split, drift, sparkle on our kids' extended tongues.
Poison, yes—but how can we confess, this moment
a glimmer of ghost dance for the ripening days
grandma packed us all in a taxi to pick mulberries
growing in the prairie she called her friend's backyard.
Even then, we cabbed it: no skipping, traipsing,
gallivanting in pinafores through knee-high weeds
on pathways nobody had trod before. We were modern.
Took the nighttime shimmer of fireflies for granted.
Hammered ragged nail holes into the lids of mason jars.
captured frogs and let 'em dry. Say, anyone here
seen a jumpfrog lately? Not the saucy poster frogs
making the circuit of nature museums. Or the catalog
frogs you can order in bulk and slit open, belly to jaw.
Or the five-legged flukes, lunging and falling and lunging
sidelong in burning bogs. Not those, but the hearty bulls
who advertised their longing, who puffed up
and peed in your berry-stained hands. They're gone
so suddenly: who will taste and swallow the night?

KIM ROBERTS

Prime Hook

The sharp tang of decay preserved in salt.
A narrow strip of gravel shoreline.
High tides that breach disintegrating bulkheads.
Jetties and seawalls that fail to hold the land in place.

A narrow strip of gravel shoreline
shifts with the push of tides, currents, and wind.
Jetties and seawalls attempt to hold the land in place
but millions of cubic yards of sand

shift with the push of storm surge and strong winds.
The conjunction of a full moon and high tide
means millions of cubic yards of sand
can be displaced. As sea levels rise

the conjunction of a full moon and the high tide
inundates beach grass and sand pea.
As sea levels rise, water displaces
thickets of bayberry and red cedar.

Beach grass and sand pea flood.
The arkosic sands of the alluvial plain,
home to thickets of bayberry and red cedar,
cease to breathe. The Army Corps of Engineers

bulldozes feldspar sands. The alluvial plain
sinks; the delicate vascular tissue of wetlands
ceases to breathe. The Army Corps of Engineers'
projects get wiped away by a single storm.

The delicate vascular tissue of wetlands
sinks as high tides breach broken bulkheads.
Beaches get erased by a single storm,
the sharp tang of decay preserved in salt.

ALAN SEMERDJIAN

The Coyotes of Los Angeles County

spring from the invisible
hunger of all that's hidden

outside of homes, these pairs
of sighs bright as angels'

wings, wild as wind on fire.
Two lovers walk their dog

to pass some time, daylight
heat lifting, mountain dreams

descending, the witching hour
of everything out of sight.

These are dangerous days.
The smoke from the Lake,

Saddle Ridge, Salt, and Creek,
Woolsey, Bobcat, tongues

of flame, the ghosts above
the hills sending everything

that breathes down, down, down
to survive. The lovers hold

each other close. The dog
is barking, the smell of fear,

smoke still circling the mind
licking the landscape drier.

The coyotes are here now, in
the corner of the parking lot

beneath where strangers line
the freeway, arms outstretched

looking hope in the eye, asking
not for forgiveness but why.

MARTHA SILANO

Letter to a Post-Apocalyptic Cockroach

with apologies to Matthew Olzmann

You probably think we hated frost, rime, grout, hail, icy rivers,
icy glaciers, icy shelves keeping icy glaciers
from plunging into the sea. Probably,

you think we hated gorillas, orangutans, Edith's checkerspot, the
    nine-spotted lady beetle
as much as we loved Toyota Tundras, Styrofoam coolers, Starbucks lids,
the fluorocarbons in our extra-hold Aqua-Net.

Knowing every minute what we were doing, metric ton by metric ton,
I bet you think we were incapable of dancing wildly in the aisles
at a what's-left-of-the-Dead show, but you'd be wrong.

Back then, when we still had the Amur leopard, a whopping total of
    eighty-four
because poachers killed them for their bones, steeped them in
    rice wine,
sold it as medicine. When we still had

Western red cedars, sword fern, Oregon grape, salal, twinflower,
    inside out flower,
queen's cup, red huckleberry, and the one-sided pyrola. Man, did we
    ever admire
the 44,000-mile migration route of the Arctic Tern. Hard to believe,

but there were seasons. Skiing. Low-lying vacation homes. Cities
      named Manhattan,
New Orleans, Miami. Grass died in the summer, turned emerald
      in September.
Do I have to tell you it wasn't all panic or worry? That some, in protest,

threw soup at famous art, but pretty much the days went on as they
      always had
while headlines shared the Antarctic was warming five times faster
than the global average? What were we doing,

I guess you want to know. Combusting our engines. Turning up
      the thermostat.
Paying eight cents, at the checkout line, for a paper bag. Buying stuff,
then donating it to the Global South, or tossing it into methane-

seething landfills. The ocean warmed 1.5 degrees, which to many
      seemed piddly
(most didn't know water expands as it warms). Polar ice sheets thinned.
Gail-force winds caused concrete piers to pound into each other,

collapse. Rivers fell from the sky while we fought hard for our freedom
to eat beef whenever we liked. And then we were gone. And then
(am I right?) the Earth sighed, broke into a blissful smile.

SUSANNE MOSER

extinction crisis

in this world
where every day
uncounted friends,
too many to name —
furred, feathered and free —
offer themselves,
their sounds and gestures
their gifts known and unknown
their wild presence
to our senses.

in this world
where every day
150 species stop singing,
flying, swimming, hunting
mating, breathing,
and blooming
forever.

in this world
where beauty
and blindness
live side by side
as staggering witnesses
to our day-to-day lives.

you need a fluid heart.
you need to learn how
to flow between ecstasy

and grief, between love
and the endangerment of love
so as to go on
and do the one thing
that needs to be done.
to give life
the one chance
it wants for itself:
to go on.

CINDY VEACH

Earth's Selfie with the Smooth Handfish, Now Extinct

The smooth handfish walked on hand shaped flippers,
had a Mohawk-like head fin, bulbous eyes and a perpetual

grimace that made it look badass. Like me, it preferred
a small range mostly staying close to home, sitting

on the ocean floor watching what swam by.
Never in its wildest dreams did it suspect

the lovely sea star would do it in. Who can know
what will end us, turn *now here* into *nowhere?*

When they came for the scallops the handfish had no inkling.
The boats passed overhead and patterns on their hulls

shimmered. Above them the heavens and beyond the heavens
stars, planets and other life forms—

but I don't want to travel far or hurt anything. I just want
to survive on what I can forage in my own benthic zone.

In the lens of my mind I sit on the bottom, in the sediment,
in the sub-surface layers, satisfied with what is there,

what is before me which is everything I care about
and need to live. The truth of the handfish took two hundred years

to reach me. Truth is like that. Sometimes it takes a turn,
takes a journey like Ulysses and becomes a mythic adventure

that only makes sense in another time. The scallops
were innocent. They gave everything of themselves

and when they were plundered the sea stars found
they could proliferate beyond all expectation

and why shouldn't they. They gobbled up everything
the smooth handfish needed to live and the handfish

never suspected. It kept keeping house far down
at the bottom and didn't even try to rise up

or be seen. It liked shadows, liked having a floor
to walk on amid all that water, a little sea corner

to itself. Who can deny that sea stars are stunning.
The way their arms sparkle with jewels, the way

they regenerate. I have only so many limbs
and I can't grow back what I've lost.

The lines: "The smooth handfish walked on hand-shaped flippers,/ had a mohawk-like head fin, bulbous eyes/ and a grimace that made it look badass" is taken, with permission, from the article, "Ten Facts About the Smooth Handfish, Now Extinct," from Daniel Hudon's newsletter, The Delightful Holiday, December 1, 2021.

ERIKA SPANGER

On Hope

It was the reefs at first. I can see your face:
kaleidoscopic dreamscapes of infinitesimal architects,
a biologic blockbuster that suddenly must end. You said:
tell me there's another galaxy with coral.

It was the bears too, but you don't say so.
Apex beasts in white, prowling the ice at the top of the world
(You said: Milky Way, top that) are a done deal and somehow
cliché, so you spare yourself the mocking of your broken child heart.

It was them and the rest and suddenly was everything
that makes the world shimmer and always made you know
why you came here from dark nothing.
You once walked through a world of wounds
but wounds are for healing. You walk now through
a world of ghosts, half not yet knowing
they are the dead.

(Until the toad climbs from the cloud forest muck to chirp
his springtime call and no one in the wide universe answers.
You said: then he knows, and I thought I glimpsed a ghost of you.)

You felt it grow thin. You started to grieve to rage and sometimes to panic,
looking for the door or the way off this ride. You felt it tear. And suddenly
it was too late. All those fights, long and frantic, were over
and lost. And then you didn't feel it at all. It was gone,
sublimated from your soul like vapor from ancient ice.

But listen: It's not that easy to lose hope.

In English we say "hope springs eternal."
In Russian it's "hope dies last." It's the same unbidden pulse.
In this world, if you love anything,
You hope.
You move. You press. You keep. You don't even get to decide.

You can watch the leaves fall from your hope:
a bird here, a town there; a glacier, its river, their people.
Sometimes you hear it on the radio, in thick traffic and you urgently
scan the fuming hardscape for something to make sense.
Sometimes you know because you wait in season, in place
and it never arrives, arrested en route. And the leaves fall
until all hope's branches are beautiful bones before a gathering sky.

But don't be fooled: There's more to hope than that.

However weak you see it, or dead you think it, or hard you mourn it,
this hope thing endures in the dark where deep roots sense scorched
    earth and,
blind and silent, but with the unrelenting green-fuse force of life, dig
    deeper still.

However frail you think it, whatever name you call it, hope will
    not—can not—quit.
It relinquishes, shapeshifts, detaches from the object of its desire.
And hews only but so closely to its driving spark. And therein lies
    hope's
unstoppable power: If you love anything you hope.

Not for this, not for that. That was then. Your hope has since
    mutated and evolved.
You stopped saying: I'm going to have to hope for the best. Now,
    you say:
I'm going to have to fight like hell.
And that's the bad news. You're going to have to fight like hell

without hope of "winning."
There's no winning anymore when so much is lost.
There's only what remains.

But look: It's still beautiful. I'll fight for that.

Whatever you fought for, whoever's in your locket,
the fight is now for what is left.
That is all. And that is everything.
And you, my weary friend, will never stop.

MARK SPITZER

Mindblowing

That always thought
in the back of the mind:

that we have cars
and farms and jungles and seas
with humans and birds and carbon dioxide
plus all that other stuff
including music and philosophy
and Cheez Whiz and history
rather than
          the alternative

but what would that
alternative be?

and how could anything
else really be?

     Anyway
after half a century
this question just
ceased to be

because you can't keep asking that
without ever getting
an adequate answer

unless, that is
you can live with narratives

that simplify
existential
complexities

     and if that's who you are
don't call me.

ELLEN TAYLOR

Heat

The warmth of bodies nestled in tangled sheets,
babies on mother's breasts, one hand holding another,
their pulses generating a third beat. Heat, the embrace
of friends reuniting, of saying goodbye. Heat: the hearth,
the crackle of birch bark and apple boughs flaming
in the wood stove, blue tongues of driftwood roaring,
warming up the room.

Heat— *Pack it, run from it, turn it up.* Heated conversations,
hot heads, and fiery tempers. Heated moments that end
with sirens and jail cells. Heated decisions that begin with pride
and end with regret. *The Heat is on, Take the Heat or Get out
of the kitchen.*

Heat— A careless match, unintentional match, no match
for a dry Redwoods floor, corpses of Sequoias, Ponderosa Pines,
Incense Cedar, charred and crucified. Walls of flame, rooms of fire,
No longer Paradise but a sort of hell on earth.

Heat— Acres of fish washed up on shore, thick as seaweed;
manatees starving, their sea lettuce wilted;
coral reefs dying, sharks migrating, ticks and moths
and plagues of insects never before seen in the north.

Heat— Urban heat islands of asphalt and concrete,
Caribbean islands battered by hurricanes, parched by drought,

seawater leaching into aquifers, casualties of rising seas,
waves of rain and walls of wind.

Heat— the sort generated by panels tilted towards the sun
like sunflowers, the sort made by wind-blowing turbines in wheat fields
and on platforms in the sea. Electric heat that propels busses and trains.
Warm Heat— the kind fanned by compromise and agreement.
Beneficence, which generates its own benign heat that could
cool a temper, a room, or a state, maybe even a planet.

Climate Eden

If snow, then may the wolf rule and rule benevolently.
If sea, then may the whale reign; may the sirens sing.

If land, then may the mountains go on living, telling their stories.
If us, then may death teach and teach absolutely.

The stranger asked: what has kept you from singing?
I had no answer save for this melody within me, rising and rising.

LESLEY WHEELER

Return Path

The only way to pray is through my feet,
earthward, jolted in return by the fizz
of a spiking current. I never thought a circuit

would loop through me, believed I was separate,
alone, done with gods, but here it is:
I've found a way to pray. Through my feet,

I reach down. There's something animate,
mycelial, that touches me back. It's a species
of love, a thinking-spike, a zinging circuit

of energy and dirt, blood and spirit—
plutonic conversation, mostly wordless.
The way I've found to pray is through my feet,

sole bared to wooden boards, or rug, or slate,
or buggy grass, just as you want to press
skin to a beloved's, sparking a current, a circuit.

Not that earth loves me, exactly. Matter's what
matters. She wants me to return the mess
of my only body, pray from head through feet
as I sink, unthinking ash, into love's circuit.

KATE CELL

Sonnet for the Seasons: New England

And what if we could stop it, after all,
   could stop the change too swift for us to grasp,
   listening instead to the maple's sweet dusk
drip in the metal bucket? The whip-poor-will-

may never summer here again. Recall
   to us Lock's Pond, ice thick enough to rasp
   through to snatch the drowsy trout, the chilled clasp
of hands raw in glazed wool gloves. How small,

how petty our accounting of the world
   in all its flames. We have no means to measure
   the beauties we have lost, burnt, broken—
our love shies away from our grief, we lie curled
   in shame. How should we learn now what we treasure?
   Wait. Only wait, for the windflower to open.

LEANA WEISSBERG

Landscapes

Summer is the first full season of my mom's absence
She died one week before the end of spring
In St. Louis, where I grieved, we still experienced remnants of the season
A biblical rainstorm and humid afternoons giving way to cool nights
I seem to recall that fire season had already begun in California,
Though I know I'm misremembering
It's just that the conflagrations seem too epic, too all-consuming, to
    ever not have been
happening
To have a beginning or an end
The scale would have been unimaginable just a few years ago
The entire breadth of the Sierra Nevada
Burned over in the span of two months
The first time in recorded history
And then, a few weeks later, the second
But this is no sudden change
The pot has been working to a boil
I know, some fire is good fire, and not every acre burned is gone
But somehow this year, it's all hitting differently
The implication, the psychoanalysis, the indelible truth
Is that the death of my mother was its own natural disaster
And each day that I see a looming column in the too near distance
I'm reminded of the tumult, the loss, and the dislocation still
    churning inside me
Clear, cloudless days stir up roiling emotions,
Inconceivable leaps of imagination, fear, anger, and anxiety that defy
    containment lines
Then come days when a gray haze smothers all feeling and
    everything stays static,

for better and for worse.
No growth
No expansion
In those in between moments, when I have enough presence of
    mind to think without
spiraling into Joan Didion's vortex, I ask myself:
How will this place feel six months, a year from now?
When will this landscape of loss transform into one of healing?
And what will that look like?
Will I be at peace with the wounds of my grief — the cat face scars
    that laid me bare?
Will I relish the newfound vulnerability they bring?
Or will I be glad for their occlusion?
Will I gaze in wonderment as my psyche greens up?
Noticing less what's missing, but what its absence made space for?
Can I wait patiently — ten years, twenty, or more — for regeneration?
Which durable parts of myself will survive, or even be buttressed?
Will I learn to weather losses, destruction, uncertainty, unraveling?
Will I shed what doesn't serve me?
Fear, anxiety, the products of so much wasted time and energy
Will these appendages die suddenly, like an epiphany?
Or will they fall away, slowly, by attrition?
Can I accept resilience as a process?
Can I receive whatever version of this landscape it might produce?
And on whatever timeline it needs?
Will I accept the default position, that these scars and shifts are
    symbols of loss?
Or can I will them to be symbols of survival?

WENDI WHITE

The Long View

Imagine the Acacia
with soft sloped boughs
and the Baobabs
with towering trunks
conspired on our descent
from their heights so we'd stand
on our own, free our hands
from their limbs and wonder
what we might grasp
beyond the grassland.

We all know the lure
of a sharp horizon.
Once glimpsed,
its pull, its whiff
of adventure conjures dreams
of sweeter fruit.

Once grounded,
we thought we'd never be treed again,
but then all our roaming,
settling, building, multiplying
knocked us off our axis.

Now we see the woods
whole: root reaching root,
trees sheltering saplings,
birds delivering seed like mail.
Hypha web of fungal sharing

binding blossom and worm,
berry and bee, a world
woven toothy and thick,
nothing separate in itself.

Imagine that we were sent
to the savanna on ancestral assignment.
After all, Humans and Ficus share
a quarter of our genes.

Imagine the trees
doing the math, betting on us
to return for instruction

DENISE WILCOX

Breach

When I flew to Alaska
And sailed through the clouds,
Closer to heaven than the landing strip,
I whispered a prayer,
Three wishes,
To Kiyaghneq,
The Way of Life.

A glacier.
A whale.
A wolf.

Let me hear the whiplash crack
Of a calving glacier and watch
A mountain of ice fall into the sea.
Let me feel mist on my cheeks
As a humpback whale breaches
Through churning waves,
Stretches skyward, then falls
Backward into the joy of the bay.
Let me watch a gray wolf,
Wild and free,
Lope across the tundra
Soaked in autumn's red and gold.

Before it is too late.
Before the sun melts the glaciers,
Before the water warms too hot for whales,
And before wolves fall to extinction.

Kiyaghneq answered my prayers.
My body plunged with the glacier into pristine water.
My body soared with the whale through the blue.
My body mirrored the proud gait of the wolf.
Not even poets possess words
For the awe of these wonders.

The People of Kiyaghneq, Siberian Yupik,
Are one with their brothers and sisters of The Land.
But not so the marauders of the Klondike Calamity.
The Reckless People gashed deep scars into Earth.
Slashed forests. Overkilled. Rushed to ruin.

When my grandchildren seek adventure in Alaska,
Seek the ineffable wonders of the glacier, the whale, the wolf.
When they long to follow The Way of Life,
Will Kiyaghneq have the power to answer their prayers?

BRIAN SONIA-WALLACE

Crown of Flames

I would
run but
I am
a forest

so I wait
while long-
tongued flames
lick lost leaves.

I seal seeds
in resin
to melt
with heat

so after
I am
a burnt husk
new pines

that have lain
dormant for decades
will sprout
through ash.

I would
run but
I am
a planet

so I wait
while ants
tunnel & monkeys
build rockets

& fall in love
& everything
burns but
not everything

is lost.

 This poem was set to music by noted composer Saunder
Choi, commissioned by The L.A. Choral Lab. Scan the QR
code to view the recording as an additional way to engage
with the poetic text.

AUTHOR'S NOTE:

*Pyrophytic plants are species that have evolved to not only withstand, but take
advantage of, fire. California's native giant sequoias are one such species. These
trees, which can grow over 300 feet tall and live over 3,000 years, need their forests
to burn in order to dry pine cones and release seeds for new growth.*

*Ironically, the species is endangered because European-derived forestry practices of
fire suppression, coupled with drought and climate change, have led to a build-up of
dry fuel in their forests. This causes uncontrolled blazes and has destroyed up to 20%
of the total population in the last decade alone.*

*It may be too little, too late, but contemporary best practices look to native land
use practices, with controlled burns, as a remedy. Rather than seeing humans, and
fire, as separate from nature — something to be kept out in order to preserve
pristine wilderness — these new/old practices acknowledge the interconnectedness
of our species.*

ERNESTO L. ABEYTIA

L'Oceanogràfic de València

Your memory echoes the pier's gasps,
rousing the ocean's waves.

A penguin sobs in the distance.
Lines of coral discharge out of sight.

I am a frosted seahorse
bound to wisps and instinct.

Encourage me to recede from turmoil.
Encourage me to refuse my dreams.

Below is a sea turtle planting seeds
in the world's grassy disorder.

Above us, two white feathers lift the sky,
meet hearty fruit and mixed rinds.

If I return, I'll carry this world like a pearl,
not the black stone it has become, loose of stability.

AFTERWORD

by Sam Illingworth

Dear Human at the Edge of Time: Poems on Climate Change in the United States is a timely and important anthology that sheds light on the climate crisis. While science and scientists play a crucial role in understanding the causes and effects of our changing climate, they are not the only ones responsible for mitigating against them.

Everyone has a role to play in addressing this urgent issue, including individuals, governments, businesses, and organisations. It is important that we all take responsibility for reducing our carbon footprint, supporting sustainable practices, and advocating for policies and initiatives that prioritise environmental protection. By working together, we can make meaningful progress in mitigating the impacts of this crisis and ensuring a sustainable future for ourselves and future generations.

Poetry has a unique ability to inspire and mobilise people in ways that traditional scientific reports and data cannot. By using language, imagery, and metaphor to connect readers to the natural world and the impact on communities, poetry can create a sense of shared purpose and urgency in addressing the issue.

For example, a poem that vividly describes the impact of a drought on a community could inspire readers to take action to conserve water or support initiatives to combat climate change. In this way, poetry can help catalyse collective action against the climate crisis by bringing people together and inspiring them to take meaningful steps towards environmental protection and sustainability.

This anthology is a powerful reminder of the role that poetry can play in addressing the climate crisis. As the co-editors of this collection, Luisa A. Igloria, Aileen Cassinetto, and Dr Jeremy Hoffman have brought together a group of poets whose work speaks to the lived experiences of what these changes have wrought in the United States and beyond.

Through their poems, these writers bear witness to the impact of the climate crisis on communities across the country. They remind us that these effects are not abstract or distant, but rather are felt in the day-to-day lives of people in every corner of the nation. Their words challenge us to confront the urgent need for action and to demand a more just and sustainable future.

I am inspired by the power of poetry to move us, to challenge us, and to connect us to one another and to the natural world. *Dear Human at the Edge of Time* is a testament to the vital role that poetry can play in raising awareness of the climate crisis and in spurring us to action. As the afterword for this collection I invite you to re-read these poems, listen to their voices, and then join in the urgent conversations and actions in addressing environmental justice that they so eloquently evoke.

Dr. Sam Illingworth is an award-wining science communicator and Associate Professor at Edinburgh Napier University in the UK, where his research involves using poetry to engender meaningful dialogue between scientists and society. Sam is also poet, game designer, Chief Executive Editor of *Geoscience Communication* and founder of *Consilience*, the world's first peer-reviewed science poetry journal. Find out more about his work via his website www.samillingworth.com.

ACKNOWLEDGMENTS

The editors are grateful for the opportunity to offer this anthology as a companion to the congressionally mandated Fifth National Climate Assessment (NCA5), a report to the president and Congress that "analyzes the effects of global change on the natural environment, agriculture, energy production and use, land and water resources, transportation, human health and welfare, human social systems, and biological diversity."

This anthology, which grew out of the National Poets Laureate civic projects, was made possible with support from the San Mateo County Office of Arts and Culture, San Mateo County Arts Commission, and the Academy of American Poets and Mellon Foundation's poet laureate initiative.

Very special thanks—

—to our advance readers especially Dr. Claire Wahmanholm, Dr. Sam Illingworth, Renato Redentor Constantino, Deputy Chair of the Expert Advisors to the Climate Vulnerable Forum, and book designer C. Sophia Ibardaloza;

—to Poets for Science/Wick Poetry Center at Kent State University for developing the interactive microsite *Dear Human*;

—to Dr. Jessica C. Whitehead and the Institute for Coastal Adaptation and Resilience, Old Dominion University, for seeding some of the important early connections for this project;

—to Allison Crimmins and Allyza Lustig of the U.S. Global Change Research Program, and Amy Stolls and Jessica Flynn of the National Endowment for the Arts for providing guidance and promotional support;

—to Dr. Linda Rugg, Professor in the Scandinavian Department at UC Berkeley; Tiff Dressen and the Staff at the UC Berkeley Office of Research; Bruce Riordan and the Berkeley Climate Change Network; the Clarion Performing Arts Center; the South San Francisco Public Library; the San Francisco Public Library; Elizabeth River Trail; Elizabeth River Project and the Ryan Lab; Philippine American Writers and Artists, Inc.; Midwest Climate Resilience Conference; New England Poetry Club; Soul

Bone Literary Festival; Mechanics' Institute; Nueva School; the University of Nebraska-Lincoln; Skyline College; the Exploratorium; and the American Geophysical Union for hosting our first book events;

—to our U.S. Poet Laureate Ada Limón, and to Vaughan Fielder and Fred Courtright of The Permissions Company, for granting permission to reprint "And, Too, The Fox," which first appeared in *The Hurting Kind*, Milkweed Editions, 2022;

—to Aimee Nezhukumatathil for granting permission to reprint "Triggerfish Invective," which first appeared in *Kenyon Review* Volume 44, Number 4, July/Aug 2022;

—to Lee Ann Roripaugh for granting permission to reprint "#sandhillcranes #string of beads," which first appeared in *The Account*, Issue 9, Fall 2017;

—to Alan Semerdjian for granting permission to reprint "The Coyotes of Los Angeles County," which first appeared in the winter 2022 issue of *The Coachella Review*;

—to Martha Silano for granting permission to reprint "Letter to a Post-Apocalyptic Cockroach," which first appeared in *Cutthroat 28*;

—to Angela Narciso Torres for granting permission to reprint "Harvesting the Heart," which first appeared in *The Best American Poetry* blog, August 2, 2019;

—to Brian Turner for granting permission to reprint "Hyperion," which first appeared in *The Wild Delight of Wild Things*, Alice James Books, 2023;

—to Claire Wahmanholm, for granting permission to reprint "P," which first appeared in *Meltwater*, Milkweed Editions, 2023;

—to Khaty Xiong for granting permission to reprint "Aubade," which was a Finalist in the 2022 Montreal International Poetry Prize;

—to Ernesto L. Abeytia, Bradley Allf, Anna Sims Bartel, Kristin Berkey-Abbott, Mary Grace Bertulfo, Amanda M. Blake, Dave Bonta, Cassandra Bousquet, Allen Braden, Cynthia Buiza, Kate Cell, Eva Chen, Everett Cruz, Natalie Damjanovich-Napoleon, Sofia Fall, Molly Fisk, Mary Fitzpatrick, Eric Forsbergh, Sue Davis Gabbay, Lee Anne Gallaway-Mitchell, Gail Giewont, Caitlin Gildrien, Annette Boushey Holland, John Hoppenthaler, Catherine Hulshof De La Peña, E.W.I. Johnson,

Melinda Koyanis, Marisa Lin, Karen Llagas, Katharyn Howd Machan, David S. Maduli, Kindra McDonald, Joshua McPeak, Mac Mestayer, Claire Millikin, Rajiv Mohabir, Heidi Mordhost, Susanne Moser, January Gill O'Neil, Calvin Olsen, Craig Santos Perez, Jeanine Pfeiffer, Ngoc Pham, Alice Plane, Kyle Potvin, Aman Rahman, Chelsea Rathburn, Sheri Reda, Kim Roberts, Ellen Sander, Emily Schulten, Jordan Steven Sher, Kim Shuck, Brian Sonia-Wallace, Erika Spanger, Mark Spitzer, Eileen R. Tabios, Ellen Taylor, Sony Ton-Aime, Cindy Veach, Leana Weissberg, Lesley Wheeler, Wendi White, Denise Wilcox, Maw Shein Win, and Diana Woodcock, for granting first serial rights to publish their work.

It is our hope that this anthology will give us pause and move us to inspire more stories of climate justice and resilience—to be kinder and do better.

CONTRIBUTORS

Ernesto L. Abeytia is a Spanish-American poet and teacher. His poems appear or are forthcoming in *Nine Mile, Lake Effect, DIALOGIST, Prairie Schooner, Fugue, Crab Orchard Review*, and elsewhere. He holds an MFA in Creative Writing from Arizona State University, an MA in English from Saint Louis University, and an MA in Anglo/North-American Cultural and Literary Studies from the Autonomous University of Madrid in Madrid, Spain. He currently teaches at Binghamton University and Arizona State University.

Bradley Allf is a postdoc at North Carolina State University studying ecology. He also works as a freelance science writer and his work has appeared in a variety of publications, including *Smithsonian, Sierra, Undark, Atlas Obscura* and *Scientific American*. Bradley studied creative writing at the University of North Carolina at Chapel Hill and has worked as an editor for the literary magazine *In Layman's Terms*.

Once described as "part activist, part administrator, and part academic," **Anna Sims Bartel** earned her Ph.D. in Comparative Literature at Cornell and has worked at the intersection of higher education and public life, including most recently co-editing *The Scholar as Human: Teaching and Research for Public Impact*, from Cornell University Press. Her interests all center on making the world a healthier, more beautiful place, which is also how she came to poetry. While trained in criticism, argument, and refutation, she now devotes herself to connecting, caring, and creating.

After earning a Ph.D. in English, **Kristin Berkey-Abbott** has published a wide variety of individual short stories and poems, along with three larger collections of poems: *Whistling Past the Graveyard* (Pudding House Publications), *I Stand Here Shredding Documents*, and *Life in the Holocene Extinction* (both published by Finishing Line Press). She has spent decades in higher ed, as a teacher and an administrator, and now she is experiencing higher ed as an MDiv student at Wesley Theological Seminary, while continuing to teach college level English classes.

Mary Grace Bertulfo has written for television and children's education at CBS, Pearson Education Asia, and Schlessinger and for the magazines *Sierra* and *Chicago Wilderness*. Her fiction, essays, and poetry have appeared in

Growing Up Filipino II, Our Own Voice, City of Big Shoulders and others. She has an MA in cultural anthropology from UC Berkeley and an MFA in Fiction from Southern New Hampshire University where she was the Orion scholar and was awarded the Lynn Safford Memorial Prize. Mary Grace founded Banyan: Asian American Writers Collective in Chicago where she paddles rivers and meanders prairies.

A cat-loving daydreamer and mid-age goth who loves geekery of all sorts, from superheroes to horror movies, urban fantasy to unconventional romance, **Amanda M. Blake** is the author of such horror titles as *Nocturne* and *Deep Down* and the fairy tale mash-up series *Thorns*. amandamblake.com

Dave Bonta (davebonta.com) is a web publisher from central Pennsylvania, best known for the poetry film site movingpoems.com. Print collections include *Ice Mountain* (Phoenicia Publishing, 2017) and *Breakdown: Banjo Poems* (Seven Kitchens Press, 2013). He's currently engrossed in ecopoetic mapping of the local and regional landscape, in between making erasure poems from every entry in the *Diary of Samuel Pepys.*

Cassandra Bousquet is a student at Roger Williams University in Rhode Island and a graduate of the Youth Climate Ambassadors program, a youth leadership program centering around climate education and activism in San Mateo County, California. Her work is featured in the collaborative poem, "Breathe," which appeared in *Nature & Culture 2021 Festival Book* (Copenhagen: Red Press Kulturhuset Islands Brygge & Københavns Kommune, 2021). She held the position of Linden Place Writer-in-Residence for the month of April, 2023 in Bristol, Rhode Island.

Allen Braden is the author of *A Wreath of Down and Drops of Blood* and *Elegy in the Passive Voice*. His poems have been anthologized in *The Bedford Introduction to Literature, Poetry: An Introduction, Best New Poets, Spreading the Word: Editors on Poetry, Cascadia: A Field Guide through Art, Ecology and Poetry* and *The World Is Charged: Poetic Engagements with Gerard Manley Hopkins*. He lives near the historic site of Fort Steilacoom in Lakewood, Washington.

Cynthia Buiza is the former Executive Director of the California Immigrant Policy Center (CIPC). She earned a master's degree in International Affairs from the Fletcher School at Tufts University, with a concentration on human security studies. She also holds certificates from the Harvard Kennedy School of Government and the Stanford Graduate School of Business. Cynthia currently serves as a California State Commissioner with the Little Hoover Commission and the CA100. Her poems have appeared in various anthologies and publications in the Philippines and the US. Her debut poetry collection, *The Future Is a Country I Do Not Live in*, was released by Paloma Press in August 2022.

Kate Cell is the Senior Climate Resilience Campaign Manager for the Climate & Energy program at the Union of Concerned Scientists. Kate leads a multi-disciplinary team of scientists, policy analysts, legislative affairs staff, and outreach and communication experts working to achieve policies that can reduce global warming emissions and increase resilience to climate change impacts. She holds a BA from Macalester College, studied at the Iowa Writers' Workshop, and lives in the Robert Frost poem that is Shutesbury, MA.

Eva Chen is the founder of *Footprints on Jupiter*, a teen literary magazine, which raised funds for the World Literacy Foundation. Her work has been recognized by the Scholastics Art and Writing Competition, and featured across *The Offing*, *Cathartic Literary Magazine*, *Catcher Zine*, *Elan Literary Magazine*, and KALW radio. She was named Burlingame's Youth Poet-in-Residence and San Mateo County Young Woman of Excellence in 2022, and will be attending Yale University in the fall of 2023. When she's not writing, she's either rewatching Avatar or trying her hand at philosophy!

Everett Cruz (he, they) is a multicultural Filipino-American who grew up in Fort Worth, Texas. He lives and teaches in Denton, Texas. His writing has been or will be published in *The Bitchin' Kitsch*, *Resurrection Magazine*, *Dipity*, *Marias at Sampaguitas*, *Stanza Cannon*, and *Five South*. @EverettCruzIsOK

Natalie Damjanovich-Napoleon is an Australian-American writer and educator who is currently completing a Creative Writing PhD on erasure poetry and forgotten histories. Her work has appeared in *Cordite*, *Meanjin*, *Australian Poetry Journal* and *Writer's Digest*. She has won the Bruce Dawe Poetry Prize (2018) and KSP Poetry Prize (2019). She has taught writing workshops in the U.S. and Australia and helped run a volunteer poetry reading series, Voicebox Fremantle. Her debut poetry collection *First Blood* was released in 2019. Her second poetry book, *If There Is a ButterflyThat Drinks Tears*, will be released in late 2023 by Life Before Man Books.

Sofia Fall is a writer from Michigan. She has an M.A. in Climate & Society from Columbia Climate School, and works in climate communications and policy, most recently for the Red Cross Red Crescent Climate Centre.

Molly Fisk edited *California Fire & Water, A Climate Crisis Anthology*, with a Poets Laureate Fellowship from the Academy of American Poets. She's the author of *The More Difficult Beauty*, *Listening to Winter*, and *Everything But the Kitchen Skunk* among other books and has won grants from the NEA, the California Arts Council, and the Corporation for Public Broadcasting. Fisk lives in the Sierra foothills, where she provides weekly commentary to community radio, and works as a radical life coach. Visit her at mollyfisk.com and www.patreon.com/mollyfisk

Mary Fitzpatrick's poems have been finalists for the Joy Harjo Poetry Prize and the Slapering Hol Chapbook Award; featured in *Mississippi Review*, *Atlanta Review* and *North American Review* as contest finalists; and published in such journals as *Agenda* (UK), *Briar Cliff Review*, *Cholla Needles*, *Hunger Mountain*, *International Literary Quarterly* (*InterLitQ*), *The Paterson Review*, *Pratik*, *Red Canary*, *Silver Birch Press*, *Spillway*, *Terrain*, *West Trestle Review* plus eleven anthologies. A graduate of UC Santa Cruz with an MFA from UMass Amherst, she is a fourth-generation Angeleno who lives in Pasadena and feels at home in Ireland.

Eric Forsbergh's poetry has appeared in JAMA, *The Journal of Neurology*, *Streetlight*, *Artemis*, *The Northern Virginia Review*, and multiple other venues. A retired health care provider, he has participated in medical mission trips to Guatemala and Appalachia, and was a volunteer COVID vaccinator for his county public health department. He has completed a Master's level certificate in social justice from the John Leland Center for Theological Studies, and is in training to teach in prisons. He is a Vietnam veteran.

Sue Davis Gabbay can usually be found reading or writing. She aspires to be an artist whose medium is words, preserving beautiful or unique moments to share with others or to carry into the future. She has published two books of poetry and several chapbooks. Born in Virginia, she grew up in southern Indiana; in retirement she has returned to Virginia. She holds an AB degree from Indiana University and an MLS from Syracuse University; she has attended several poetry workshops in recent years.

Lee Anne Gallaway-Mitchell lives and writes in Tucson, where she received an MFA in creative writing from the University of Arizona. Her essays have won *The Florida Review* Editor's Award, the Arts & Letters Susan Atefat Prize for Creative Nonfiction, and most recently, the *Boulevard Magazine* Nonfiction Contest for Emerging Writers. She is at work on a memoir, *Campfollowers*.

Gail Giewont chairs the Literary Arts Department at Appomattox Regional Governor's School for the Arts and Technology in Petersburg, Virginia. Her poetry chapbook *Vulture* is available from Finishing Line Press.

Caitlin Gildrien is a writer and visual designer living on a two-hundred-year-old farmstead at the feet of the Green Mountains, on Abenaki land that once was the bottom of an ancient sea. Her work has appeared in *Tampa Review*, *The Rumpus*, *Rattle*, *Poets Reading the News*, and more. Her first book of poems is looking for its home.

Annette Boushey Holland's writing has appeared in *Streetlight Magazine*, *Spindrift: Stories of Place*, *The Wind Horse*, and other publications. She holds an MA in English Literature and taught English composition. A former staff writer for the Nature Conservancy, Annette helped found two land trusts and is working to protect redwood forest in Northern California.

John Hoppenthaler's books of poetry are *Night Wing over Metropolitan Area*, *Domestic Garden*, *Anticipate the Coming Reservoir*, and *Lives of Water*, all with Carnegie Mellon UP. With Kazim Ali, he has co-edited a volume of essays on the poetry of Jean Valentine, *This-World Company* (U of Michigan P). Professor of English at East Carolina University, he also serves on the Advisory Board for Backbone Press, specializing in the publication and promotion of marginalized voices.

Catherine Hulshof De La Peña is a Chicana ecologist from San Antonio, Texas. She is currently a professor at Virginia Commonwealth University. She studies the responses of plants and butterflies to climate change across mountains of Virginia, Costa Rica, and Puerto Rico. She is also a recipient of the prestigious Early Career Faculty Award from the National Science Foundation.

E.W.I. Johnson is a poet living and working in Chicago. He is currently earning his MFA at Northwestern University, and has poems published or forthcoming in *Lone Mountain Literary Society*, *Snarl*, and *Sonora Review*.

Melinda (Mindy) Koyanis is a decades-long Cambridge, MA resident, now retired from her career at Houghton Mifflin and Harvard University Press as Director of Intellectual Property. Mindy has participated as artist, creator, and audience with several university and community-related organizations. Mindy holds a Juris Doctor from Suffolk University Law School and B.A. from Boston University.

Ada Limón is the author of six books of poetry, including *The Carrying*, which won the National Book Critics Circle Award for Poetry. Her book *Bright Dead Things* was nominated for the National Book Award, the National Book Critics Circle Award, and the Kingsley Tufts Poetry Award. Her work has been supported most recently by a Guggenheim Fellowship. She was the host of the critically-acclaimed poetry podcast, The Slowdown. She grew up in Sonoma, California and now lives in Lexington, Kentucky where she writes and teaches remotely. Her new book of poetry, *The Hurting Kind*, is out now from Milkweed Editions. She is the 24th Poet Laureate of the United States.

Marisa Lin is a daughter of immigrants and Minnesota native. She is a 2023 Poetry Fellow at UC Berkeley's Arts Research Center, with work in *Poetry South*, *Lucky Jefferson*, *Porter House Review*, *The Racket*, and elsewhere. Her chapbook, DREAM ELEVATOR, will be published in 2024 by Kernpunkt Press. Marisa is pursuing a Master's Degree of Public Policy at UC Berkeley.

Karen Llagas's new chapbook, *All of Us Are Cleaved*, was released by Nomadic Press in 2023. Her first collection of poetry, *Archipelago Dust*, was published by Meritage Press in 2010. A recipient of a RHINO Founder's Prize, Filamore Tabios, Sr. Memorial Poetry Prize & a Hedgebrook residency, her poems have also appeared in various journals and anthologies. She lectures at UC Berkeley, and divides her time between San Francisco and Los Angeles.

Katharyn Howd Machan, an enthusiastic professor in the Department of Writing at Ithaca College, has served as coordinator of the Ithaca Community Poets and director of the Feminist Women's Writing Workshops, Inc. Her poems have appeared in numerous magazines, anthologies, textbooks, and collections (most recently *Dark Side of the Spoon* from the Moonstone Press in 2022 and *A Slow Bottle of Wine*, winner of the Jessie Bryce Niles Chapbook Competition, from Comstock Writers, Inc. in 2020), and she has edited three thematic works, including *Adrienne Rich: A Tribute Anthology* with Split Oak Press. For body and spirit, she belly dances.

David S. Maduli is a father, husband, poet, educator and descendant of migrants from the Philippines. His work, often inflected by his years as a DJ and public school teacher, has received the Joy Harjo Poetry Prize, National 1st Runner-Up for The Inlandia Institute's Hillary Gravendyk Prize, and residencies and fellowships with Las Dos Brujas, VONA, Martha's Vineyard Institute of Creative Writing, and Napa Valley Writers' Workshop. Born in San Francisco, he is a longtime resident of Oakland, Lisjan Ohlone land, where he completed his MFA at Mills College with a fellowship in Community Poetics. In addition to his work in public schools, he is an instructor in the MFA in Writing program at Lindenwood University.

Kindra McDonald is a poet-artist and author of *Teaching a Wild Thing*, *Fossils* and *In the Meat Years*. She was the recipient of the 2020 Haunted Waters Press Poetry Award. She received her MFA from Queens University of Charlotte. She works in mixed-media and found poetry and teaches at The Muse Writers Center in Norfolk. She served as the Poetry Society of Virginia Southeastern VP from 2019-2022. You can find her in the woods or at www.kindramcdonald.com

Josh McPeak is a freshman Literary Arts major at Appomattox Regional Governor's School in Petersburg, Virginia.

Mac Mestayer is an experimental physicist recently retired from Jefferson Lab, a national accelerator center for nuclear physics located in Newport News, Va. His research focused on the quark structure of protons and neutrons. His hobbies include hiking, bird-watching, wood sculpture and poetry. He lives In Williamsburg, Va. with his wife Kathi.

Claire Millikin is the author of nine books of poetry, including *Dolls* (2Leaf Press 2021), *Transitional Objects* (Unicorn Press 2022), and *Elegiaca Americana* (Littoral Books 2022). Millikin now lives in rural, coastal Maine, and teaches Art History and American Studies for the University of Maine and for Bates College. Millikin is a 2021 recipient of the Maine Literary Award.

Rajiv Mohabir is the author of three collections of poetry including *Cutlish* (Four Way Books 2021) which was awarded the Eric Hoffer Medal Provocateur, longlisted for the 2022 PEN/Voelcker Prize, and was a finalist for the National Book Critics Books Award. He also authored the memoir *Antiman* (Restless Books 2021), winner of the Forward Indies Award for LGBTQ+ Nonfiction, and was a finalist for the 2022 PEN/America Open Book Award, 2021 Randy Shilts Award for Gay Nonfiction, and 2021 Lambda Literary Award for Gay Memoir/Biography. As a translator, his version of *I Even Regret Night: Holi Songs of Demerara* (Kaya 2019) won the Harold Morton Landon Translation Award from the Academy of American Poets in 2020. His fourth poetry collection *Whale Aria* is forthcoming in September 2023 from Four Way Books.

Heidi Mordhorst is the author of two collections of poetry for young readers and contributions to journals and anthologies for both adults and children, most recently *Poetry by Chance* (ed. Taylor Mali, Button Poetry 2023) and *Imperfect II* (ed. Tabatha Yeatts-Lonske, 2022). She taught in public schools for 35 years, leading many Green School initiatives, and recently served on the NCTE Excellence in Poetry Award Committee. She now offers poetry enrichment programs through her organization WHISPERshout Writing Workshop, and advocates for climate rescue policy through many local organizations in Montgomery County, MD.

Susanne C. Moser (she/her) is an independent scholar and consultant who works in the US and internationally from a base in western Massachusetts, the unceded ancestral homeland of the Nipmuc and Pocumtuc. A geographer by training (Ph.D. 1997, Clark University), her work over the past 30 years has focused on adaptation to climate change, climate change communication, science-policy interactions, and psycho-social resilience in the face of the traumatic and transformative challenges associated with climate change. She has served on scientific advisory boards for Future Earth, the International Science Council, the US National Research Council and contributed to various reports of the IPCC. She also served on the Federal Advisory Committee to the Third US National Climate Assessment and co-led its coastal chapter. Her mostly unpublished poetry is inspired and infused by the nature beings around her — owls calling before sunrise, wild cats under the waning moon, red leaves on a furious October wind. You can learn more about Susi's work at www.susannemoser.com.

Aimee Nezhukumatathil is the author of the illustrated nature essay collection, *World of Wonders: In Praise of Fireflies, Whale Sharks, & Other Astonishments*, finalist for the Kirkus Prize in non-fiction, and named the 2020 Barnes and Noble Book of the Year. She is also the author of four books of poetry, and is poetry editor of *Sierra*, the national magazine of the Sierra Club. Awards for her writing include The Ohioana Award in non-fiction, a Kansas Book Award, fellowships from the Mississippi Arts Council, Mississippi Institute of Arts and Letters Award for poetry, National Endowment of the Arts, and the Guggenheim Foundation. Her writing has appeared in *NYTimes Magazine*, *ESPN Magazine*, and twice in *Best American Poetry*. She is professor of English and Creative Writing in the University of Mississippi's MFA program.

Calvin Olsen holds an MFA from Boston University and recently completed his PhD in Communication, Rhetoric, and Digital Media at NC State University. His work has appeared in *The Adroit Journal*, *AGNI*, *Couplet Poetry*, *The National Poetry Review*, and *SAND*, among many others, and his translation of Portuguese poet João Luís Barreto Guimarães's ninth collection, *Mediterranean*, was published by Hidden River Press earlier this year. More can be found at calvin-olsen.com.

January Gill O'Neil is an associate professor at Salem State University, and the author of *Glitter Road* (forthcoming, 2024), *Rewilding* (2018), *Misery Islands* (2014), and *Underlife* (2009), all published by CavanKerry Press. From 2012-2018, she was the executive director of the Massachusetts Poetry Festival. Her poems and articles have appeared in *The New York Times Magazine*, the Academy of American Poets' Poem-A-Day series, *American Poetry Review*, *Poetry*, and *Sierra* magazine, among others. The recipient of fellowships from the Massachusetts Cultural Council, Cave Canem, and the Barbara Deming Memorial Fund, O'Neil was the 2019-2020 John and Renée Grisham Writer-in-Residence at the University of Mississippi. She currently serves as the 2022-2023 board chair of the Association of Writers and Writers Programs (AWP).

Craig Santos Perez is a Pacific Islander writer from Guam. He is the author of five poetry collections, most recently *Habitat Threshold* (2020). He is a professor of English at the University of Hawai'i at Manoa, where he teaches Pacific literature and eco-poetry.

Jeanine Pfeiffer is an ethnoecologist focusing on biocultural diversity: the intrinsic connections between nature and culture. Her award-winning essays, research articles, poems, and films have been nominated for the Pushcart Prize, anthologized, broadcast over radio, exhibited in art galleries, and published in major media outlets, literary magazines, and scientific journals. @JeaninePfeiffer and jeaninepfeiffer.com

Ngoc Pham is a Vietnamese poet currently living in the United States. They are a recipient of the Academy of American Poets College & University prize and a finalist for the *Adroit Journal* poetry contest. They are planning on attending an MFA program in Creative Writing in Fall 2023.

Alice Plane focuses on the various stakes that climate change poses to the planet's ecosystems, including human societies, with a specific focus on equity. She has worked in France, Madagascar and Afghanistan, assuming roles as a humanitarian and aid program officer, consultant, diplomat for France and the EU. From 2016 to 2020, she coordinated international climate negotiations within the French ministry of Foreign Affairs. She served as an expert reviewer for the IPCC.

Kyle Potvin's debut full-length poetry collection is *Loosen* (Hobblebush Books, 2021). Her chapbook, *Sound Travels on Water*, won the Jean Pedrick

Chapbook Award. Her poems have appeared in *Bellevue Literary Review*, *Tar River Poetry*, *Ecotone*, *The New York Times*, and others. She is a peer reviewer for *Whale Road Review*. Kyle lives on the Seacoast of New Hampshire.

Aman Rahman is a Muslim poet from Long Island, NY. He currently attends Stony Brook University where he serves as an editor of the undergraduate journal, *Sandpiper Review*. His work has been published in *Narrative* and *Consequence*.

Chelsea Rathburn is the author of three poetry collections, most recently *Still Life with Mother and Knife*. Raised in Miami, Florida, she now lives in Macon, Georgia, where she teaches at Mercer University and serves as Poet Laureate of Georgia. In 2021, she received an Academy of American Poets Laureate Fellowship to create Georgia Poetry in the Parks, seasonal poetry trails placing poems in the paths of Georgia parkgoers.

Sheri Reda is a writer, presenter, and performer from Chicago whose Italian escaped Italian peasantry to tend impossibly verdant gardens in their industrial backyard. Her written work has appeared in *The Examined Life Journal*, *The Healer's Burden*, *Spirit*, *Haiku Quarterly*, and other journals. Her presentations have found audiences at the CG Jung Center, the Wilmette Library, and several narrative medicine conferences.

Kim Roberts is the editor of the anthology *By Broad Potomac's Shore: Great Poems from the Early Days of our Nation's Capital* (University of Virginia Press, 2020), selected by the East Coast Centers for the Book for the 2021 Route 1 Reads program as the book that "best illuminates important aspects" of the culture of Washington, DC. She is the author of *A Literary Guide to Washington, DC: Walking in the Footsteps of American Writers from Francis Scott Key to Zora Neale Hurston* (University of Virginia Press, 2018), and six books of poems, most recently *Corona/Crown*, a cross-disciplinary collaboration with photographer Robert Revere (WordTech Editions, 2023). www.kimroberts.org

Lee Ann Roripaugh (she/they) is a biracial Nisei. Her fifth volume of poetry, *tsunami vs. the fukushima 50* (Milkweed Editions, 2019), was named a "Best Book of 2019" by the New York Public Library, selected as a poetry Finalist in the 2020 Lambda Literary Awards, cited as a Society of Midland Authors 2020 Honoree in Poetry, and was named one of the "50 Must-Read Poetry Collections in 2019" by Book Riot. They are the author of four other volumes of poetry: *Dandarians* (Milkweed, Editions, 2014), *On the Cusp of a Dangerous Year* (Southern Illinois University Press, 2009), *Year of the Snake* (Southern Illinois University Press, 2004), *Beyond Heart*

Mountain (Penguin, 1999), and a chapbook, *#stringofbeads* (Diode Editions, 2023). She was named winner of the Association of Asian American Studies Book Award in Poetry/Prose for 2004, and a 1998 winner of the National Poetry Series. Their short story collection, *Reveal Codes*, was recently selected as winner of the 2023 Moon City Short Fiction Award, and will be forthcoming from Moon City Press in late 2023. The South Dakota State Poet Laureate from 2015-2019, Roripaugh is a Professor of English at the University of South Dakota, where they serve as Director of Creative Writing and Editor-in-Chief of South Dakota Review. Roripaugh served as one of the jurors for the 2021 Pulitzer Prize in Poetry, and was appointed as the Mary Rogers Field and Marion Field-McKenna Distinguished Professor of Creative Writing at DePauw University for spring 2022.

Ellen Sander (she/her), a rock and roll heart, has had work published in *Vogue*, the *NY Times*, the *New Yorker*, *Georgia Review*, *Sonic Boom*, *Cabildo Quarterly* and loads of other venues. Her book, *Trips, Rock Life in the Sixties* has been reissued in an augmented edition by Dover. Her poetry chapbook, *Aquifer*, is published by Red Bird Chapbooks. *Hawthorne, A House in Bolinas* is published by Finishing Line Press. A New York City native, she's lived in South Salem, Bolinas, L.A., Beijing and is now cohabitating with eagles and chickadees in Belfast, Maine. This poem is dedicated to her grandchild Ezra (they/them) and their generation of Earthlings.

Emily Schulten is the author of two poetry collections, most recently
The Way a Wound Becomes a Scar, a 2023 Eric Hoffer Award Finalist, and her poems appear in *Ploughshares*, *Kenyon Review*, *Prairie Schooner*, and *Alaska Quarterly Review*, among others. She is currently a professor of English & creative writing at The College of the Florida Keys.

Alan Semerdjian is an Armenian-American writer, a musician, and an educator. Recent recognitions include two Pushcart Prize nominations; a Frontier New Poets Award; poems in *Poetry International*, *The Brooklyn Rail*, and *Fence* (forthcoming); and a tweet from Kim Kardashian that made his 2020 spoken word album *The Serpent and The Crane* (with guitarist/composer Aram Bajakian) viral for a day. Alan's poem "The Writing About It Again" was part of a short, animated film ("An Armenian Triptych: Retracing Our Steps," made in collaboration with Bajakian and artist Kevork Mourad) that was selected for and a finalist in several film festivals in 2021-2022. Pulitzer Prize winner Peter Balakian has called his first full-length poetry collection, *In the Architecture of Bone* (GenPop Books, 2009), "well worth your reading." Alan has been teaching English in public schools for the past 25 years while recording, releasing, and touring in support of several critically-acclaimed collections of music across a range of genres. He is on the advisory board for the International Armenian Literary Alliance, through which he founded and directs the Young Armenian Poets Awards.

Jordan Steven Sher is the author of *And Still We Rise: A Novel about the Genocide in Bosnia* (2021). His previous book, *Our Neighbors, Their Voices: True Stories of Immigrant Exodus*, was published in 2019. He just completed a manuscript of historical fiction that is based on the early life of a Sephardic Jewish boy who escaped transport to a death camp, and fought for the Yugolslav Partisans during World War II, to be published later this year. As a second generation older-American, he has witnessed the evolution of a crumbling democracy in the U.S. that warrants a laser focus on saving the planet first, and convincing climate deniers and most corporations that our existence is in the balance. jordanstevensher.com

Kim Shuck was born in San Francisco, California, and is a member of the Cherokee Nation of Oklahoma. She received a BA in Art and an MFA in Textiles from San Francisco State University. Shuck is the author of *Noodle, Rant, Tangent* (Andover Street Archives Press, 2022), *Exile Heart* (That Painted Horse Press, 2021), *Murdered Missing* (FootHills Publishing, 2019), *Deer Trails* (City Lights Books, 2019), *Clouds Running In* (Taurean Horn Press, 2014), *Rabbit Stories* (Poetic Matrix Press, 2013), and *Smuggling Cherokee* (Greenfield Review Press, 2005). In 2019, she was awarded an inaugural National Laureate Fellowship from the Academy of American Poets, and a PEN Oakland Censorship Award. She served as the 7th poet laureate of San Francisco.

Martha Silano is the author of five full-length poetry books. Her most recent collection is *Gravity Assist* (Saturnalia Books 2019). Previous collections include *Reckless Lovely* (2014) and *The Little Office of the Immaculate Conception* (2011), also from Saturnalia Books. Martha's poems have appeared in *Poetry*, *Paris Review*, *Poetry Daily*, *New England Review*, *American Poetry Review*, and *The Best American Poetry* series, among others. She teaches at Bellevue College.

Brian Sonia-Wallace is a queer, bilingual poet and cultural worker interested in themes of intimacy, service, debt, queerness, grief, authorship, memory, and transcendence. He is the West Hollywood City Poet Laureate, a 2021-22 Academy of American Poets Laureate Fellow, and the author of *Maze Mouth* and *The Poetry of Strangers: What I Learned Traveling America with a Typewriter*. His long-term project RENT Poet invites the public to share their stories in exchange for poems about them, written in real-time on a vintage typewriter. Brian runs a monthly queer open mic at Micky's WeHo and was once quote-tweeted by Bjork.

Erika Spanger, the Director of Strategic Climate Analytics in the Climate and Energy program at the Union of Concerned Scientists, researches, writes and speaks about U.S. climate change vulnerability, impacts and just resilience. She currently manages UCS's climate impacts analyses, work that helps shed light through new research, analysis, communication and outreach on ongoing and accelerating climate harm, current efforts to adapt to this change, and the urgency of strong leadership and action.

Mark Spitzer is the author of 31 books, most of them about "monster fish" and our shared environmental concerns. He is also a professor of creative writing somewhere in Arkansas. More info at sptzr.net.

Eileen R. Tabios has released over 70 collections of poetry, fiction, essays, and experimental biographies from publishers in 10 countries and cyberspace. In 2023 she released the poetry collection *Because I Love You, I Become War* and an autobiography, *The Inventor*. Other recent books include a first novel *DoveLion: A Fairy Tale for Our Times*; and two French books, PRISES (Double Take) (trans. Fanny Garin) and *La Vie erotique de l'art* (trans. Samuel Rochery). She created the hay(na)ku, a 21st century diasporic poetic form; the MDR Poetry Generator that can create poems totaling theoretical infinity; and the "Flooid" poetry form that's rooted in a good deed. Translated into 12 languages, she also has edited, co-edited or conceptualized 15 anthologies of poetry, fiction and essays. Her writing and editing works have received recognition through awards, grants and residencies. More information is at http://eileenrtabios.com

Ellen M. Taylor is a professor of English at the University of Maine at Augusta, where she coordinates language and literature programs and regularly teaches in the prison education program. In Maine, she organizes the annual Plunkett Maine Poetry Festival, held each April in Augusta. She is the author of three collections of poetry, *Floating* (2009), *Compass Rose* (2015), and recently, *Homelands* (2022). Taylor has published scholarship on Maine women writers Celia Thaxter, Elizabeth Coatsworth, and Kate Barnes, considering intersections between gender, language, and ecology. She lives in Appleton, Maine.

Sony Ton-Aime is a Haitian poet, essayist, and translator. He is the Michael I. Rudell Director of Literary Arts at Chautauqua Institution. He is the author of the chapbook, *LaWomann* (Ironworks Press, 2019), the Haitian Creole translation of the book *Olympic Hero: The Lennox Kilgour's Story*, coauthor of the Haitian Creole course on Duolingo, and co-founding editor of ID13. His work has appeared and is forthcoming in *Artful Dodge*, *La Revista PingPong*, *The Oakland Review*, *Dunes Review*, Poets.org, *The Idaho Review*, *Hunger Mountain Review*, *Cleveland Review of Books*, among others.

Angela Narciso Torres is the author of *What Happens Is Neither* (Four Way Books 2021), *Blood Orange*, winner of the 2013 Willow Books Literature Award for Poetry, and the chapbook, *To the Bone* (Sundress Publications 2020). Recent work appears or is forthcoming in *POETRY*, *Missouri Review*, *Quarterly West*, *Cortland Review*, and *Poetry Northwest*. A graduate of Warren Wilson MFA Program for Writers and Harvard Graduate School of Education, Angela has received fellowships from Bread Loaf Writers' Conference, Illinois Arts Council, and Ragdale Foundation. She received First Prize in the Yeats Poetry Prize (W.B. Yeats Society of New York). New City magazine named her one of Chicago's Lit 50: Who Really Books in Chicago. Born in Brooklyn and raised in Manila, she currently resides in San Diego. She serves as a senior and reviews editor for *RHINO Poetry*.

Brian Turner is a writer and musician, with five volumes of poetry and a memoir, *My Life as a Foreign Country*. "Hyperion" is part of *The Wild Delight of Wild Things* (Alice James Books, 2023). He's the editor of *The Kiss*, and co-edited *The Strangest of Theatres*. His work has been published in *The New York Times*, *The Guardian*, *National Geographic*, *Harper's*, and other fine journals. Turner was featured in the documentary film "Operation Homecoming: Writing the Wartime Experience," nominated for an Academy Award. He lives in Orlando with the world's sweetest golden retriever, Dene.

Cindy Veach is the author of *Her Kind* (CavanKerry Press), a finalist for the 2022 Eric Hoffer Montaigne Medal, and *Gloved Against Blood* (CavanKerry Press), a finalist for the Paterson Poetry Prize and a Massachusetts Center for the Book 'Must Read.' Her poems have appeared in the Academy of American Poets Poem-a-Day, *AGNI*, *Michigan Quarterly Review*, *Salamander*, *Poet Lore* and elsewhere. Cindy is the recipient of the Philip Booth Poetry Prize and the Samuel Allen Washington Prize. She is co-poetry editor of MER (Mom Egg Review). cindyveach.com

Claire Wahmanholm is the author of *Meltwater* (2023), *Redmouth* (2019), and *Wilder* (2018). Her work has most recently appeared in, or is forthcoming from, *Cream City Review*, *TriQuarterly*, *Sierra*, *Ninth Letter*, *Blackbird*, *Washington Square Review*, *Copper Nickel*, and *Beloit Poetry Journal*. A 2020-2021 McKnight Writing Fellow, and the winner of the 2022 Montreal International Poetry Prize, she lives in the Twin Cities.

Leana Weissberg is a Research Fellow at the UC Berkeley Center for Law, Energy & the Environment, where she applies her background as a forester to issues at the intersection of climate change and wildfire resilience. Leana is a nearly native Californian living in the Sierra Nevada foothills with her partner and pup.

Lesley Wheeler is the author of the hybrid memoir *Poetry's Possible Worlds*; the novel *Unbecoming*; and five books of poetry, most recently *The State She's In*. Her poems and essays appear in *Poetry*, *Kenyon Review Online*, *Poets & Writers*, and *Guernica*, and she is Poetry Editor of *Shenandoah*.

Wendi White is a poet and educator now musing among the geckoes and ginger scented ridges of O'ahu after a recent relocation from the continental US. She earned her MFA from Old Dominion University's Creative Writing program in Virginia. In 2022, she was nominated for a Pushcart Prize by the Red Rock Review. When not at her writing desk, she can be found shooing Giant African Land Snails from her garden.

Denise Wilcox lives in Keswick, VA. Family is her joy and nature is her peace, whether hiking National Park trails or watching her pollinator gardens thrive. She is an award-winning author who writes poetry and nonfiction for all ages. Her work has been published in *The Poetry Society of Virginia's Centennial Anthology*, *Paterson Literary Review*, *Ladybug*, *FunforKidz*, *Quilted Poems*, the Society for Children's Book Writers and Illustrators journal *Highlighter*, and *Developmental Medicine and Child Neurology Journal*.

Maw Shein Win's most recent poetry collection is *Storage Unit for the Spirit House* (Omnidawn) which was nominated for the Northern California Book Award in Poetry, longlisted for the PEN America Open Book Award, and shortlisted for CALIBA's Golden Poppy Award for Poetry. Win's previous collections include *Invisible Gifts* (Manic D Press) and two chapbooks *Ruins of a glittering palace* (SPA) and *Score and Bone* (Nomadic Press). Win's Process Note Series features poets and their process. She is the inaugural poet laureate of El Cerrito, CA and teaches poetry in the MFA Program at the University of San Francisco. Win often collaborates with visual artists, musicians, and other writers and was recently selected as a 2023 YBCA 100 Honoree. mawsheinwin.com

Diana Woodcock is the author of seven chapbooks and five poetry collections, most recently *Holy Sparks* (2020 Paraclete Press Poetry Award finalist) and *Facing Aridity* (2020 Prism Prize for Climate Literature finalist). A three-time Pushcart Prize nominee and a Best of the Net nominee, she is the recipient of the 2022 Codhill Press Pauline Uchmanowicz Poetry Award (for her sixth full-length manuscript, *Heaven Underfoot*), the 2011 Vernice Quebodeaux Pathways Poetry Prize for Women (for her debut collection, *Swaying on the Elephant's Shoulders*), and the 2007 Creekwalker Poetry Prize. Currently teaching at VCUarts Qatar, she holds a PhD in Creative Writing from Lancaster University, where she researched poetry's role in the search for an environmental ethic.

Khaty Xiong is the author of the full-length poetry collection, *Poor Anima* (Apogee Press, 2015), and three chapbooks: *Ode to the Far Shore* (Platypus Press, 2016), *Deer Hour* (New Michigan Press, 2014), and *Elegies* (University of Montana, 2013). Her honors include a Ruth Lilly & Dorothy Sargent Rosenberg Poetry Fellowship from the Poetry Foundation, residencies at MacDowell, a Vermont Studio Center Fellowship from the Ohio Arts Council, and two Individual Excellence Awards from the Ohio Arts Council. Xiong's work has been featured in the following publications: *Poetry*, *The New York Times*, Poetry Society of America and Academy of American Poets websites, and elsewhere. In 2018, her poem, "On Visiting the Franklin Park Conservatory & Botanical Gardens" was highlighted in an immersive poetry installation at the Poetry Foundation Gallery in Chicago, a collaboration between the Poetry Foundation and the Smithsonian Asian Pacific American Center, centering on the conversation of grief and loss. In 2019, she was awarded Best of the Net for her poem, "Year of the Cardinal's Song (VII)." She was the Spring 2022 Artist-in-Residence at the Asian/Pacific/American Institute at NYU.

EDITORS

Originally from Baguio, Philippines, **Luisa A. Igloria** is the author of numerous books of poetry, including *Maps for Migrants and Ghosts* (Southern Illinois University Press, 2020), co-winner of the 2019 Crab Orchard Poetry Prize, and the chapbook *What is Left of Wings, I Ask*, winner of the Center for the Book Arts Letterpress Poetry Chapbook Prize selected by Natasha Trethewey. In 2015, she was the inaugural winner of the Resurgence Prize (UK), the world's first major award for ecopoetry. A Louis I. Jaffe Professor and University Professor of English and Creative Writing, she teaches in the MFA Creative Writing Program at Old Dominion University which she directed from 2009-2015. Dr. Igloria also leads workshops at The Muse Writers Center in Norfolk, and was appointed Poet Laureate of the Commonwealth of Virginia 2020-22, Emerita. In 2021, she received an Academy of American Poets Laureate Fellowship.

Aileen Cassinetto was named an Academy of American Poets Laureate Fellow in 2021 and YBCA 100 honoree in 2023 for her contributions in building regenerative and equitable communities through poetry. Her ecopoetry projects were featured in Copenhagen's Nature & Culture Poetry Film Festival, Lift-Off Filmmaker Sessions, and in Americans for the Arts' *Arts Link* magazine. She is the author of two poetry collections, and her work has appeared in *American Poets*, *Poetry*, and poets.org, among others. The founder of Paloma Press, she currently serves as Arts Commissioner and Commissioner on the Status of Women for San Mateo County.

Jeremy S. Hoffman is the Director of Climate Justice and Impact at Groundwork USA and an Affiliate Faculty in the L. Douglas Wilder School of Government and Public Affairs and the Center for Environmental Studies at Virginia Commonwealth University. He specializes in Earth science communication, data-driven and community-based participatory science, and has years of experience developing experiences for science center exhibitions. Most recently, Dr. Hoffman was appointed Chapter Lead for the Fifth National Climate Assessment, and served the Science Museum of Virginia as their Climate and Earth Scientist, completing the requirements of a three-year NOAA Environmental Literacy Grant. Visit jeremyscotthoffman.com to find out more about his work, research, and science communication.

www.ingramcontent.com/pod-product-compliance
Lightning Source LLC
Chambersburg PA
CBHW030957210726

48290CB00007B/2355